from the]
(Part of the

PERCEPTIONS, PARABLES, and POINTERS

What do you really want to do with your time? What is your mission in life? Where have you been, and where would you like to go? What are your dreams, your hopes, your wishes? If you could do anything in the world, what would it be?

JERALD SIMON

To my **sweetheart**, Zanny, with all my love.

Dedicated to the greatest minds from
the beginning of time to the present.

Motivation at its Best.

Music Motivation®
http://musicmotivation.com

PERCEPTIONS, PARABLES, and POINTERS
by JERALD SIMON

Music Motivation®, **http://musicmotivation.com**
P.O. Box 1000 Kaysville, UT 84037-1000 U.S.A.
info@musicmotivation.com; +1-801-444-5143

Copyright © 2017 by JERALD SIMON

For more promotional excerpt permission, contact:
Music Motivation®
P.O. Box 1000 Kaysville, UT 84037-1000
http://musicmotivation.com
info@musicmotivation.com

International Standard Book Numbers (ISBN)
Paperback - 978-0-9980785-1-9
eBook - 978-0-9980785-2-6
Audio Book Barcode - 190394009274
Library of Congress Control Number: 2016915821

Also available as an Audio Book, MP3 on iTunes, Amazon, CDBaby and all online music retailers. Visit your favorite online music retailer to download the MP3 audio book read by Jerald Simon.

Printed in the **United States of America**
Simon, Jerald
Jerald Simon's Perception, Parables, and Pointers by Jerald Simon
Edited by Suzanne Simon and Wendy Cederlof

Motivation at its Best.

TABLE OF CONTENTS

Create a table of contents for your life. Pretend for a moment you are creating a personal time-line for the years between your birth and death (which is a new birth or beginning in and of itself). What would the table of contents look like? What would the main headings and chapter titles be?

Your life is a table of contents and the contents of your life are, can, and will be what you make it. Make the most of your own personal table of contents. Write the best selling, epic version of the greatest life you'd like to live and then follow your handbook through life. Live your life to the fullest and enjoy each chapter of *your* life!

JERALD SIMON

http://musicmotivation.com
http://youtube.com/jeraldsimon
http://facebook.com/jeraldsimon
http://linkedin.com/in/jeraldsimon
http://twitter.com/jeraldsimon

"My purpose and mission in life is to motivate myself and others through my music and writing, to help others find their purpose and mission in life, and to teach values that encourage everyone everywhere to do and be their best." - JERALD SIMON

First and foremost, Jerald is a husband to his beautiful wife, Zanny, and a father to his wonderful children. Jerald Simon is the founder and president of Music Motivation®. He is a composer, author, poet, and Music Mentor/piano teacher (primarily focusing his piano teaching on music theory, improvisation, composition, and arranging). Jerald loves music, teaching, speaking, performing, playing sports, exercising, reading, writing poetry and self help books, gardening, and spending time with his wife, Zanny, and their children.

Jerald created **musicmotivation.com** as a resource for piano teachers, piano students, and parents of piano students. In 2014 he began creating his weekly "Cool Songs" to help teach music theory - the FUN way by putting FUN back into theory FUNdamentals. He is the author/poet of "The As If Principle" (motivational poetry), and the book "Perceptions, Parables, and Pointers." He is also the author of 21 music books from the Music Motivation® Series. He has also recorded and produced several albums and singles of original music.

Jerald also presents to various music schools, groups, and associations throughout the country doing workshops, music camps, master classes, concerts and firesides to inspire and motivate teens, adults, music students and teachers. He enjoys teaching piano students about music theory, improvisation, and composition. He refers to himself as a Music Mentor and encourages music students to get motivated by music and to motivate others through music of their own.

I Believe In You

from the book
The "As If" Principle (motivational poetry) (by Jerald Simon)

I believe in you. I believe in all that you can do.
I believe you're intelligent. I believe in your dreams.
I believe circumstance is irrelevant,
it never is quite what it seems.

I believe in your abilities.
I believe in your word.
I believe you'll do what you say you will do,
because I believe in you.

You are capable, you are able.
You're more powerful than you know.
You'll accomplish what you want to accomplish,
you'll learn, and improve, and grow.

I believe in your future.
I believe you will do your best.
I believe you will prosper.
I believe you will be blessed.

I believe in your talents.
I believe in your gifts.
I believe God has a purpose for you,
He inspires, prepares, and lifts.

I believe in your greatness.
I believe in your heart.
I believe you have a mission in life,
and will fulfill and do your part.

I hope you believe in yourself.
I hope you believe in your dreams.
I know you will do what you were sent here to do.
Your life is much more than it seems.

"When we fall down, we GET BACK UP!"

This book has been a very long time coming! I began writing parts of it when I was in High School at Weber High School. Other parts were written while in college at Weber State University, and later in life. Much of what has motivated me and pushed me forward in life is based on what I tell my children almost daily:

"When we fall down, we <u>GET BACK UP!</u>" If you say the first part to my children, "When we fall down", they all automatically respond with *"WE GET BACK UP!"* This encompasses not only physical falls, but mental, emotional, spiritual, financial, and all different kinds of "falls".

This ideology began when I was eight years old and had fallen off of a 50 foot cliff. I cracked my head open and the doctors put a total of 26 staples in my scalp. I endured seizures for the next year, as well as frequent doctor visits, CAT scans, and MRIs. As a result of the fall, I have no memory of my life before the accident. It is a miracle I am alive and was not paralyzed.

After my fall from the cliff, I resolved that each day would be a new birth for me regardless of how many times I would fall down, both literally and metaphorically. It helped me see that life is precious. It is a gift and should be cherished. It helped me to evaluate my priorities and focus more intently on what matters most. Now, we don't need to fall off a 50 foot cliff to get sense knocked into us, but we all need to continually have reminders and even wake up calls that help us refocus our energy into the best life has to offer us.

"No matter how many times you fall down... <u>ALWAYS</u> GET BACK UP!"

We all fall down, metaphorically, and make mistakes. We may do poorly on a school or work assignment. As a result, we may feel we don't measure up. We may feel like failures as parents, and worry that others criticize us. We might feel depressed and even apathetic toward life. At times we may feel unsure, insecure, afraid, and doubt our own abilities, potential, and future. What must happen when we fall down emotionally, spiritually, financially, and even socially? We *must* GET BACK UP!

Throughout this book, I have written my own perceptions on life. These are motivational tips and ideas to help each of us improve and strive to be better today than we were yesterday.

This book, for me, is a manual of what I would share with my younger self. It is what I would encourage myself to think and strive to become. It is something to turn to for those times when we have been beaten by the bullies of life. Life is full of intricate and unforeseeable twists and turns. The ups and downs can take their toll. The focus, however, must be on our potential and possibility! If we can believe in ourselves and hope for the best within us and within others as well, then we can commit to do and be our best. We can strive to be better because we choose to look for the best in life. Yes, there are discouraging days and moments of madness when everything that *could* go wrong *will* go wrong. That is life. We don't need to enjoy it, but when those dark days get us down, we can always GET BACK UP! It may be difficult, but it is worth it. It may take time, but is imperative to realize that we can improve and change. We cannot give up on ourselves!

Our perception of life is seen through our own understanding or misunderstanding of life, based on the experiences we have and have not had, the knowledge we have and have not acquired, and the interactions we have and have not had with those around us.

- JERALD SIMON

Perceptions

(These are my own perceptions on life)

I have presented these as individual paragraphs. Each one is completely independent of each other, though many do relate to and help explain one another. Each paragraph is an idea or perception that has been presented to help you think and focus on your own personal improvement.

I hope you enjoy reading these perceptions and insights on life. My main goal in writing down these perceptions and in creating this book in general is to present ideas that will get people thinking, imagining, planning, creating, and actively participating in life.

What do you really want to do with your time? What is your mission in life? Where have you been, and where would you like to go? Are you spending your time wisely? Are you taking advantage of every opportunity that comes your way? What are your dreams, your hopes, your wishes? If you could do anything in the world, what would it be? What are your talents? What are your aspirations? What brings *you* happiness? What kind of a life would you like to live? Do you enjoy what you do? If not, why not?

Be certain of the uncertainties in life. No matter how much you think you know, continually think about how much more you ought to and could know. Work on what you don't know. Search for knowledge. Don't just think about it, actively seek it. Knowledge empowers you with the ability to empower others. Share your knowledge with others. Help others improve and become better.

Don't tell me you're not good at something. People will always be better and worse than you at everything you do. Tell me whether or not you are making progress. If you are progressing, are you measuring your progress? If you are not progressing, why not? Get to know your strengths and your weaknesses. Develop your own personal progress plan and determine how you could improve and progress from where you are. You most likely don't know how far you have come and how much you truly have accomplished. Improve and progress!

Immerse yourself in good books. Read one to two hours per week if you can, more if time permits. Become acquainted with the literary classics. Read as much as you can on personal improvement (self help), history, people, business, and finances. Study the great works of the philosophers. Study scriptures and read about religions and anything that adds value to religious beliefs. Invest in yourself! Learn as much as you can and become a student of life. You can learn a great deal from the experiences of others, from their great successes and also from their failures. Everything you read becomes part of you. Carefully choose what you read on a daily basis. Be very careful with what you choose to read. The words you choose to read play an important role in your personal development and overall outlook on life. Be open-minded about what you read and often take what you read with a grain of salt. Much of what we read is written through colored lenses and is the summation of someone else's thought, habit, education, beliefs, and past and present life experiences.

Be proactive. Passivity is a poison. Avoid it like the plague. Actively participate in life. You are not a bystander standing on the sidelines of life. Get in the game and go for the goal. Choose what you will do with your life. Choose what you will do with your time. What will you do? What will you watch, read, accomplish, and become? Accomplishment is a result of action. Act the part. Don't pretend or put on a façade. Don't wait. Don't pause. Don't hesitate. Go. Be. Do. Accomplish. Get it done. ACT. ACT NOW!

11

Take time to stop and smell the flowers. Have a picnic. Play games and earnestly enjoy life. Have fun. Live leisurely. Learn to drive in the slow lane of life. Don't let opportunities to truly experience life pass you by, go unnoticed, or be unappreciated.

Learn from others. Study people. Get to know them. Learn from their strengths and understand their weaknesses. Read biographies about the most influential men and women throughout history. Create your own character collage where you pattern your own life after the great mentors and role models who have helped shape and mold you. Look up to others. Be teachable. Listen more and speak less. You can learn something from everyone. Don't be a know-it-all and don't think you're better than anyone else. Never stop learning.

See the world for what it is and not for what you expect or want it to be. Be realistic, but embrace optimism. The world is good, but help it be better, and personally strive to be better and do your best. Negativity is your nemesis and a needless waste.

We all have importance. This world is as meaningful as we make it. Every day we build our personal palaces piece by piece, and brick by brick. We struggle to build it but we are better off for building it. We change! We improve and grow.

How much time do you spend planning and preparing for your financial future? How much do you invest? How do you invest it? How much do you save? Annually? Monthly? Weekly? Daily? Have you decided how much you would like to earn? Annually? Monthly? Weekly? Daily? Hourly? How will you earn your wealth?

I suggest you create various multiple streams of income. Produce high quality products that inspire, entertain, and educate. Anything that will enhance or improve someone's life is valuable to them because it adds value to their life. Financial returns come when we invest in others and their needs. Put others first. Ask yourself how you can help others. Forget about your own financial problems and begin helping others. Forget about yourself. Your finances will improve.

Save 10 to 15 percent of everything you make (regardless of how much or how little you make). Create a company, produce a valuable and viable product, service, or program that makes a difference in someone's life. Follow this format until you have several products and services producing multiple streams of income. Each stream comes from existing streams and will allow you to generate more streams of income. Pay a 10 percent tithing (this is in addition to the 10 - 15 percent you save for yourself). Paying a continual 10 percent tithing allows you to give back to others. This is the law of giving: give selflessly, give without thinking of expecting anything in return, and give completely of yourself, of your time, and of your talents. Your financial rewards in life are determined by how much time you spend planning and preparing for your financial future. Produce, save, and invest. Spend a little time each week on your finances. Determine how much you would like to earn - annually, monthly, weekly, daily, and hourly.

Now that we've discussed the importance of planning and preparing for your financial future, let me simply say money is not everything and we should not be overly concerned or consumed by making or earning money, or even becoming wealthy. Now that almost completely contradicts what I wrote on the previous page. And yet, both points of view are very valid and important to understand and follow. There are much more important aspects of life and our focus should be on leaving a legacy and teaching our children and family values. These joys in life are much more important than acquiring wealth. True wealth is a compilation of humility, faith, and an understanding of who we are and what our purpose in life is and should be.

Focus on the needs of the individual. Sometimes the needs of the one far outweigh the needs of the many. The feelings, interests, perspectives, beliefs, welfare, and overall   well-being of one person cannot and should not be overlooked. If we each will focus on helping one individual improve, progress, grow, change, and be their best - the needs of the many will be met because the individual needs are being taken care of and satisfied.

Be humble. Sincerely acknowledge that you don't know everything, and you can't do everything. Accept yourself as you are. Realize you have limitations, weaknesses, bad habits, unrealistic expectations, and moments of doubt, worry, and fear. Humility helps us grow and improve. Never compare your circumstances with anyone else.

What are your talents? Are you using your talents to enrich others? Are you sharing your gifts with others? You have an opportunity to bless countless lives by giving of yourself. Let your voice be heard. Stand up and stand out.

Make time for music. Learn about different genres and types of music. Get to know the history of music. Study about composers. Learn to read music and learn how to play (and sing) music. Learn to play at least one to two musical instruments. Make music of your own. Play your instruments daily. Share your music with others. When you do so, you not only share what you love, you share yourself with others.

Set goals. Goals give you direction. Create a one year goal plan, a five year, 10 year, 15 year, and 20 year goal plan. Plan and prepare for the future. Decide what you want to learn and then learn it. Your goals will help you plot out your destination from beginning to end. Be prepared. Know what you are doing and what you will be doing at each stage of your life. Don't leave change up to chance. See what changes need to be made and then make them. Go for the goal. They are, after all, your goals. Never give up on your goals. Never give up on yourself. Keep pushing yourself to continually outdo yourself.

Eat healthy foods, a wide variety of fruits and vegetables. Drink at least 8 glasses of pure water daily. Don't overeat or eat to excess. Take care of your body or you will become unhealthy, be unable to do your ultimate best each day, and be unable to truly experience life to the fullest. Exercise daily! Get at least 6 - 8 hours of sleep daily. Walk or run at least 3 - 4 times per week (preferably daily, if possible). Be health conscious and consciously live a healthy lifestyle. Optimal health and great physical fitness go hand in hand. Work out with weights, stretch, meditate, do yoga, cardio, etc., and treat your body with the utmost respect and reverence.

Suggested Daily Workout Schedule
If this helps you, great. If not, keep doing what works for you
(you can and should always vary things).

- Lift Weights (free weights) - 15 - 30 min.
- Do 20-100 pushups
- Do 20-100 jumping jacks
- Do 20-100 crunches (or sit-ups)
- Run or walk - 15-30 min. per day
- Meditate/Stretch (morning *and* evening) - 10 min.

Recommended work out books:

For MEN: The Men's Health Home Workout Bible

For MEN: The Men's Health Big Book of Exercises

For WOMEN: The Women's Health Big Book of Exercises

There are many additional exercise books for men and women - find the one that is the best book for you - you'll know what works for you!

Listen intently. Open your ears and really listen to what others say to you. More often than not we hear only what we want to hear in a conversation. More frequently we are guilty of speaking too much and listening too little. When others speak to you, give them your undivided attention. Don't think about your responses or what you want to say. Listen to the other person and look at them when they speak. Look into their eyes. After your conversation, you should be able to identify their eye color. Listen intently to what people say verbally and non-verbally. Sometimes more can be said by a person's body language than his spoken word. Your actions say a lot about you.

Help and serve others. Selflessly give of your time and expertise. Each of us has strengths *and* weaknesses. We can learn from others and give of ourselves to help others. Don't give with the thought of getting something in return. Don't think of yourself at all. Think of *their* needs. Serve and sacrifice for the benefit of others. Remember, it's not about you. It's about others. It's not about your wants or needs. It's about theirs. Try not to speak of yourself, your ideas, or your accomplishments - speak about theirs. Listen to how frequently you use the word "I." Try to eliminate the following words from your daily vocabulary: "I," "Me," "My," "Mine," and "Myself". Take yourself out of every situation. The focus should not be about you and your world. When you focus on you, your world shrinks. When you focus on others, your world expands and your life is enriched because you strive to enrich the lives of others.

Everyone should dream. I'm not talking about daydreaming or hoping for something you and I know will never happen unless *you* do something about it - I'm talking about *dream encoding*.

When someone actively participates in dream encoding, he begins to encode his dreams deep into his DNA (so to speak, of course). He focuses so intently on his dreams on a conscious level that his subconscious not only accepts the dreams as a reality, but the dreamer begins to create a dream blue print for accomplishing his dreams. An action plan is then put into motion and their dream time-line has a deadline and various completion check points along the way.

Dream encoding is the process of turning your dreams into reality. They become part of you. Dreams are active entities that continue to grow and change as you grow and change. Our dreams foster other dreams. One dream leads to another in a never-ending and continually perpetuating dream dynasty. The offspring of our current dreams produce dreams of their own if we encourage them and give them the room they need to grow.

Dreams are very delicate and can easily be destroyed. Dreams require constant attention and nurturing care. Protect your dreams. Care for them. Help them grow and give them strength.

Compliment others. Look for the best in other people and don't be afraid to tell them how wonderful they are. Be genuine and sincere when you compliment others. Bring out the best in others. Make their day.

Become a student of life. Learn as much as you can from as many people as you can, as often as you can. There are hundreds and thousands of teachers around you at all times. Learn from your family, neighbors, co-workers, classmates, and friends (you can even learn a great deal from those who dislike you and act like enemies).

If you see someone, or know of someone being successful, regardless of what they do, ask them for advice. Ask *what* they are doing and *how* they are doing it. They will become a role model for you to follow in their footsteps. Remember, what one person can do, another can replicate and almost duplicate. You should not do exactly what they have done or do - you do need to show some creativity and originality, but use other people's successes as a guide map and a resource.

Use every successful example. Some are very successful financially, others are very successful physically, mentally, academically, emotionally, socially, spiritually, etc. Follow the successful examples of those around you. Imitate their creativity, ideas, and ingenuity. Avoid their pitfalls and faithfully follow people who are anxiously engaged in doing good. Learn life's lessons from the leaders and follow what they do. First we must be taught what the great masters and inventors know. Then we can take the wheel and invent and create our own destinies.

The eyes of the beholder are not as important as the eyes of the one being beheld. Put others and their needs before your own. Don't be concerned with yourself. Lose yourself in helping others find themselves.

Be nice to everyone. Treat everyone with respect, kindness, warmth, enthusiasm, acceptance, and great humility. Never think of anyone as your superior or inferior. Treat everyone as your equal from the humblest and destitute to the most influential and wealthy. We are a family. The human race consists of fathers and mothers, sons and daughters, and brothers and sisters - lives that connect and intertwine - individuals who learn from each other and who have an enormous amount of influence on each other's decisions.

Let it go! Whatever pains and problems have been holding you back or weighing you down - let them go. Realize, that if you let it, the past will become a perilous prison to you and will prevent you from truly enjoying the present. We can learn so many valuable and life changing lessons from the past, but if you continually re-visit the past, you will avoid and miss out on the gifts of the present. Look forward to the future in faith, but protect and preserve your presence in the present. Always be present. Let go of the problems of the past. They are behind you for a reason. Move on and make the most of each minute you have now.

One tear shed when it's meant is worth more than a thousand tears foolishly spent. Life is difficult and we need time to freely shed our tears. But don't worry about things over which you have no control. Do your part, do your best and leave everything else alone.

Pay attention to details. Focus on the finishing touches that make the ordinary become extraordinary. Fine tune your skill in noticing subtlety and simplicity. Enhance your ability to notice patterns, colors, shapes, sizes, beauty, potential, and untapped talent and hidden resources. Develop a talent for focusing intently on what others say verbally and non-verbally. Be perceptive of your surroundings. Be perceptive of others, of their feelings, their experiences, and their lives.

What have you done or are currently doing to increase and enhance your creativity? I suggest you keep daily idea notebooks and write down every idea that comes to you no matter how crazy or outlandish the ideas may be. Keep a digital voice recorder with you during the day to verbally record ideas that come to you. You should do one or all of these on a regular (if not daily) basis: (1) Create new ideas, concepts, programs, etc., (2) Create new business ideas (service/product/ventures), trademarks, copyrights, patents, etc., (3) Invent new systems, designs, technologies, schematic programs, etc., (4) Create new book ideas, book titles, movie plots, TV series, music, etc., (5) Draw, paint, act, sing, dance, perfect and perform your creations. Try doing this even if you normally don't do these things. Be in the mode of creating something. Cultivate your creativity!

Each passing day we learn and grow, for we learn about life from what others know. But when we think we know it all, we know we really haven't learned anything at all.

21

Increase your talents. To be completely honest, you can do anything - if you want it badly enough and are willing to pay the price. You are talented, but talent alone can only take you so far in life. You must learn how to work. It takes a lot of work to help someone be extremely talented. Develop a good work ethic. Do more of what works and less of what doesn't. It's just as important to work smarter as it is to work harder.

Determine what you want to do in life and then do it. You should wake up each morning refreshed, energized, and excited to face each new day. You should happily welcome the work you do each day - whether with your family, your job, your career, schooling, business, or recreational and leisure activities. It should be a delight to do what you do. If it is not - something needs to change. Either your attitude needs to improve and you need to be more optimistic and positive, or you genuinely need to re-evaluate your life and make some big changes. What is your mission in life? Why do you do what you do? What are you not doing right now that you'd like to do? What would you like to learn, know, see, do, become, experience, share, give, teach, and provide to the world? How will you do what it is you need and want to do?

An idle man dreameth of glory while a wise man putting forth the hard effort glorifies in his dreams being fulfilled. Remember, we learn more *from* a lifetime than we ever possibly could *in* a lifetime.

Soak up as much sunshine in life as you can. When you do, you will be able to spread sunshine wherever you go. See the bright side of every situation in life and make the world a little brighter by lighting up the world with your laughter, your smile, and your infectious enthusiasm. Cheerfully encourage others with your charisma and charm. Don't force it, have ulterior motives, be insincere, or unnatural in any way. Honestly be happy and smile your way through life.

Why do we speak when we have nothing to say? Think before you speak. Some people mutter the most absurd comments - voicing their offensive opinions at all times and in all places. If you think before speaking, you will decide not to say anything that will spitefully hurt or offend others. Anything said deliberately to offend, embarrass, annoy, manipulate, or put down another's opinions, thoughts, beliefs, or lifestyle should not be said. Think before you speak. Do not knowingly say anything to hurt another's feelings. Always, always think before you speak. Remember that once you have said something, it can never be taken back. You may be able to apologize for your words, but you still said them.

Sometimes we cannot expect the best until we've received the worst. The worst strengthens and prepares us to receive the best of anything. Things seem blackest before the light comes. There will always be night, but bask in the light of the moon.

Be genteel, free from vulgarity or rudeness, polite in every situation and in every circumstance. If you are a man, be a gentleman. If you are a woman, be a lady. Let your words be laced with refinement and your actions be adorned with admiration toward others. Speak kindly of all people at all times. Do not be coarse, base, lewd, or use language that is inappropriate, mean, or unbecoming of a gentleman or a lady. Be refined.

Don't pretend to be a know-it-all on the one hand, or boast of being ignorant on the other. Pseudo-intellects separate themselves from society by supposing their own superiority to others' inferiority. They view their own intellect, inflated intelligence and wisdom to exceed that of anyone else. Likewise, individuals who constantly down play their intelligence and purposefully do not perform to their full ability or potential in an effort to "fit in" or seem normal are doing a disservice to themselves and society. Do not elevate yourself or pre-suppose your understanding or intelligence to be superior or inferior to anyone elses. Each individual is doing what he can and is doing the very best he can. We must continually strive to improve, but we must not let our quest for knowledge degrade us.

A man once said, "pain comes from enduring hardships we have never endured." But, more often, we find that pain comes *not* from what we haven't endured but by continuing to do the foolish things we have done before. We must learn from our mistakes and move on.

Have a cheery disposition in life. Try to be an optimist. <u>Never</u> be a pessimist. Some people gripe and whine, grumble and groan, and complain and remain downright miserable every day. Nothing ever seems to work out for them. Everything is awful, gloomy, doomy, and depressing to them. Instead of looking for the silver lining, they see black and charcoal.

Climb out of the pit of pessimism with the ladder of laughter, an outlook of optimism and the hope of greater heights. Look for the good and you will find it. Search for serenity and be at peace with the good and the bad. Remember the phrase "this too shall pass" as you get through the difficult times.

We all experience moments of madness, we complain about our current circumstances, and ask ourselves the often heard question, "why me?" Why am I suffering? Why is this happening to me? Why did I lose my job? Why was I in this accident? Why did my relationship not work out? Why did my loved one die? The question is not "why do bad things happen to good people," the real question is what do those good people do when bad things happen to them? Do they learn from the good *and* the bad experiences of life and try to live a richer more fulfilled life, or do they stop living, hide away, and become bitter and angry? People are free to choose *how* they live, but they must live with the choices they make. When a bad choice has been made, the best thing anyone can do is to quickly right the wrong. Correct the bad situation, stop doing what shouldn't be done, and move on. Don't complain, criticize, or get angry about the current circumstances or undesirable outcome. Remember, each of our circumstances is only the result of our choices and the choices of others (both good or bad). It is only the reaction to the action. If you want a different reaction, change your actions.

Time is a rare commodity. It is priceless and invaluable. Each of us has been given 24 hours a day, 365 days a year. That equals 8,765.81277 hours or 525,948.766 minutes each year, which equals 31,556,925.9747 seconds (for those of you who enjoy exact figures - you know who you are). We alone determine what we will accomplish with the time we have been given. Our allotted time is a gift. Make the most of your time. Do not waste it. What you do with each minute cannot be undone or taken back. Once each minute is used it is gone forever. The time has come and gone and nothing you or I do can turn back the sands of time. Be careful with your time. It is very precious. It is priceless. Treasure your time. Guard it with your life and be very protective of how your time is used. Use it wisely. Use it carefully. Don't misuse it.

Make a difference in someone's life today. It could be on a grand scale such as giving sums of money to a neighbor, friend, family member, or even a stranger who needs help or assistance. It could be as simple as smiling at a stranger and saying a friendly hello. Everything you do has a ripple effect on yourself, your family, your neighbors, the community, and even the nation and the world. The chain reaction that can happen when you set out to do good is infinite. What can you give, share, and provide to and for others? Start today. Begin where you are. Make things happen. Be the difference in someone's life.

Who do you want to become? The person you were yesterday, the person you are today, and the person you can become tomorrow are all very different. You may look at the person you were yesterday and feel guilt, remorse, anger, frustration, and pity. This may even apply to the person you are today. If your past and present circumstances seem unbearable, intolerable, or undesirable in any way, you can change for the better. Decide right now to create a better you for tomorrow. Invest in yourself. Learn as much as you can about the person you want to become. How does he/she speak? What do they do, wear, know, that you don't? How do they live? What are their dreams, ambitions, plans, goals, values, etc.? Are you working on becoming who you want to become? What qualities and attributes do you need to possess? How will you obtain them? What changes could you make in your life that would be life changing? Decide to be a better person. Make the decisions you need to make today to become the person you will become tomorrow.

We are all born with many talents and wonderful gifts. The more we share these gifts, the more we in turn receive. The more we receive entices us all the more to give. Share your talents with others for their benefit, not for yours. Inspire others to share their talents as well. We each can benefit from our interaction with each other.

As a whole, the world is filled with good people who are doing the best they can to make a difference. People are generally good natured, honest at heart, looking out for each others' best interests and needs and genuinely sincere and doing the very best they can with what they have. Give people the benefit of the doubt. Be more forgiving, more tolerant, and more understanding of what they do, and even more so of what they don't. Put yourself in their shoes. Understand that roles can be reversed and situations do change. In a matter of a few moments we can find ourselves on the opposite end of the spectrum where we hope others will be more understanding of our *own* circumstances, needs, and our own shortcomings.

There are many aspects of life that are not what they appear to be. There are also many aspects of life that appear to be what they are not. You cannot judge something or someone by their appearance. Just because you think they are different, or they appear to be different, understand there really aren't that many differences that separate one individual from another. We are all made from the same mold.

Enthusiasm begets enthusiasm. It is contagious. It is the key to every success. Men and women are strengthened when they have it, weakened when they lack it, win with it, and fail without it.

Be yourself. You are uniquely original. Don't blend in with the latest fads or fashions. Stand out. Set yourself apart from others in a good way. Be the best version of you that you can be. You don't need the latest gadgets and gizmos to fit in or feel accepted by the masses. Be true to who you are.

Continually strive to increase your spirituality. The more you do to learn about God, Divinity, Mother Nature, the Universe, or whatever your belief, will help you become a better person. I believe in God so I will refer to God. Always give thanks to God. Know that life has a purpose and a plan. Whatever struggles or problems you have faced, are currently enduring, or will encounter in the future will not have been in vain. Find beauty in the world. There is beauty all around us if we will look for it and learn to appreciate it. Look to God and praise His name in your moments of triumph and success as well as during your difficulties, trials, and when you're in your own personal pit of despair. The depths to which we fall can, if we learn from them, prepare us for the heights to which we may ascend. Everything happens for a reason. We may not understand the beginning from the end, but we can appreciate divinity. Our limited understanding (or complete lack thereof) and knowledge that we don't have all the answers can help us be humble, have more faith, and increase spiritually.

Never let go of the rope of life. Keep climbing. You're not finished until you reach the top. The line of life stretches upward in a never ending journey of improvement.

Scale back. Simplicity is the best policy. We don't need so much "stuff." Our lives become cluttered with unnecessary baggage and unwanted junk. We need to consume less and produce more. If you aren't using something, get rid of it. Donate to your local thrift store or secondhand store. Give to your community. If you'd rather, you can have a yard sale. Better yet, have a "free for all trade" with your local neighbors where they can trade their unwanted stuff for yours (and vice-versa). One man's junk *is* another man's treasure. Do without or less of it. We don't need everything we think we want. Often times, once we get what we thought we wanted and feel the temporary satisfaction of obtaining and owning it, we often neglect it, forget about it, take it for granted, or do not put as much attention, focus, and energy into it after we have it as we did *before* we had it. If this is the case, whatever it is, it is being undervalued and unappreciated and would be better off with someone else. *Get rid of it!*

It's important to know the difference between your actual condition versus your desired outcome. This pertains to things as they currently are versus things as they should and could be. Examine your life and determine where you are right now and where you would like to be in the future. What is the distance between the actual and the desired lifestyle? What can you do to bridge the gap? Brainstorm and then come up with an action plan and start moving toward your dream lifestyle.

You can't see the big picture until you broaden your horizons.

Make music wherever you go. Each of us in life is a traveling musician. We share our music with others on a daily basis. Sometimes we are asked to accompany and at other times we take the lead and perform solo on the stage of life. The tempo is always changing. Sometimes we rejoice in the major events of our lives. At other times we mourn at the sadness of the minor moments we experience. There are intricate harmonies and majestic melodies that move us in meaningful ways. Life is a musical score. Each of us plays many parts as instruments in the symphony of life. In turn, we each become the composers and arrangers of our own musical masterpiece. At times, the dissonance disfigures the magical movements where melodies and harmonies intertwine and become inseparable. Share your music with others. Make music wherever you go.

Wisdom comes from taking what we have learned and applying it to real life situations. This demonstrates our understanding of what we have read, seen, heard, and observed. By applying what we have learned to the real world, we gain a greater understanding of what does and does not work. The practical application of the knowledge we have acquired improves our understanding, clarity of mind, reasoning, perception, insight, and overall ability to see a situation for what it could and should be. We must know *and* do. The one without the other creates problems, clouds our clarity of mind and judgment, and prevents us from truly experiencing real growth from doing what should be done.

It's never too late to turn around and change direction in life. As a natural result of choice, we have chosen to walk down certain paths that have either been beneficial or detrimental to our well-being. It is never too late to make a course correction and re-route our direction toward happiness, success, and personal satisfaction. If we are not satisfied with the direction we are headed we can and should turn around. Don't be afraid to go back, turn around, or start over in life.

Most people avoid opportunities because of the obligations associated with each opportunity. As one's intelligence increases so does their responsibility. The greater their capacity, the more demanding is or should be their contribution to society. Much is expected of those to whom much is given. The better educated a person becomes and strives to be, necessitates their personal outreach to help those in their community receive the best possible education they can. When an individual becomes more financially successful, he or she should seek to enrich the lives of those around them. It's about giving back to our neighbors, the community, our country, and the world. Once we have climbed out of any problematic pit, we must do everything within our power to help ourselves first, and also help those around us - family, friends, neighbors, and everyone we meet.

Follow through. If you begin something, finish it. See it through. Don't start and then stop when the going gets tough. Toughen up and roll with the punches. You can accomplish anything if you put your mind to it. You need to dream it, breathe it, think it, and speak it. Don't just talk the talk though, learn how to walk the walk. Follow through. Finish what you start.

Some people sadly and mistakenly feel they are entitled to everything. You are only entitled to the gift of your choices. What happens in between your birth and death is up to you and is a result of the choices you make. Everything you do must be earned, learned, acquired, gained, or achieved by your diligence, hard work, perseverance, sweat, sacrifice, and personal efforts. You must prove yourself to yourself and to others. Earn respect. Earn trust, integrity, and honor. Work for the money you earn. You will be compensated based on what people think you are worth. If you want to earn more money, you must learn more and do more. Be of more service. You are not entitled to anything unless you prove you have earned it.

A thoughtless thought requires no thought, while a thoughtful thought must be learned and taught. We must train our thoughts and fine-tune our thinking to carefully focus on selecting and choosing what we think about.

Perceptions, Parables, and Pointers...by JERALD SIMON

There are many stepping stones on the road to success. One of the very first steps toward success is believing in yourself. You must have confidence in *your* abilities. You must believe in *your* potential. If you don't believe you can succeed, it won't matter what you do or attempt to do in life. You must believe in yourself. Don't focus on what you can't do - focus on what you can. Don't focus on what you don't know - focus on what you do know. Stop thinking about what you have not accomplished and begin dreaming about what you will accomplish. Start your steps toward success today. Your success is only a few steps away.

Have fun. Enjoy life. Travel, explore, relax, get out and have a good time. See the world. Experience life. Get to know other parts of your city, state, nation, and the world at large. Work is wonderful, but you need to take a vacation every now and then. Play and get together with family and friends. Experience new cultures, meet new people and create many lasting friendships with people from other countries around the world. Live life to the fullest. Have fun. Enjoy life!

See what needs to be done and do it. Don't wait to be told, don't seek a reward or wait until others are watching. If you see something that needs fixing, fix it. Don't procrastinate. Go to work. Do what must be done when it needs doing. Always look for what needs to be done and do it.

Obstacles are opportunities. Realize that setbacks only temporarily suspend success. You can and will overcome any obstacle. Perseverance always produces results.

Do not dwell on defeat. Do not wallow in the well of worry or be fenced in by fear. Learn from your past mistakes and move forward. When something doesn't go as planned or you make a terrible blunder and you feel that all is lost, simply begin again. The old adage: "If at first you don't succeed, try, try, again," is as relevant today as it ever was. Mistakes can be mended. Some take more time to resolve and others less, but every problem has a solution. We may not like the solutions at first, but as every question needs an answer, every problem needs a solution.

Take a look at the problems you face each day and tackle them one by one. Ask yourself this: "Is this truly the worst that could possibly happen to me? Is it the end of the world? Is *all* lost?" After asking yourself these questions you will see the answer is no. This will never be the worst anything for you unless you dwell on your problems, bury yourself under your burdens and commit yourself to constant chastisement. If this is the case, *you* need to change. Remember, obstacles are opportunities.

Say the phrase "I'd be delighted" when asked to do any task. This phrase will strengthen and empower you. Its words will inspire you and replace any pessimistic thoughts with an optimistic outlook. No matter how difficult the challenge may be, you will become better prepared to cheerfully do what has been asked of you if you happily say, "I'd be delighted."

Do your best. Do your very best. When someone tells me they did the very best they could, and I know they honestly have done everything within their power to do their best, I don't really care about the outcome or the results. Win or lose, succeed or fail, if they have done their very best and have given it their all, then they have no reason to be disappointed, ashamed, embarrassed, or disheartened by the outcome, whatever it may be. The ones who do not do their best or give it their all, need to be concerned and worried.

You cannot coast through life. The straight A student who never studies and thinks life is a breeze will have a rude awakening when reality hits. If you are not doing your best and striving to do better, you will not experience real growth because you will never have known resistance and struggle.

Life is not a free ride and those who think it is are not living life. They can never truly be happy because they have never experienced the pain, sacrifice, work, and difficulties that teach them self-discipline, self-control, and self-mastery. Do your best. Do your absolute best and give it your all - every time, in everything you do, everyday.

Conquer thyself. Self conquest is often referred to as self-mastery, self-discipline, and self-control. We *must* control ourselves, our thoughts, our speech, our actions, and our habits (both good and bad). No one can control another person. We control ourselves and must act and not react. Do something every day to develop and strengthen your self-control. Remember, *you* are in control of you. No one else has that responsibility or privilege.

Learn to listen to music. Whether we refer to something as music or noise depends largely on our upbringing, our interests, our likes, and our dislikes. Each of us hears something different and distinct to ourselves when we listen to music. One person may hear the music, another may hear intervals, melodic movements, chord structure, tonality, harmonic progressions, etc. What we hear musically depends on our background, our study, and our personal experience. Some have more experience, some have less. Learn how to listen to music as a music enthusiast would. Think of music as a composer does. Music tells a story. What is the music telling you? Listen to the dynamics, the louds and the softs. Feel the rhythmic pulse of the piece. What is the tone of the music? Can you hear the color of the piece? Is the music thick or thin, structured or free? What is the personality of the piece? What happens to you when you listen to the music?

Everyone has ideas. We must learn how to determine which ideas are the best. Once we have selected the very best ideas, we must take them from the creative stage to the productive stage. Ideas must grow. They have their various stages of growth and development as we have ours. If they remain only in the idea stage, they will not go anywhere and nothing will change. Your mind is the "idea incubator." Define, re-define, and refine the ideas in your mind and then work to bring them to life. Don't let any idea remain in the creative stage ever. Give it birth. Give it life. Give it room to grow. Help your ideas mature and go places you only dreamed they would go. Be productive!

Sadly, some of the youth of today feel they should have something for nothing. They have grown up in a "get rich quick" society. This is what I call the "fast food" syndrome. They want the results, but do not want to pay the price. It's the lazy life. These individuals don't understand the importance or satisfaction of work well done. They have no patience for improvement because it takes time and they are impatient. We must teach our youth how to work and how to do the best work they can. We must encourage them to develop their talents. We must teach them not to give up, but to persist. Rome was *not* built in a day as they always say. Talents often take a lifetime to develop, perfect, and master. Anything worth achieving, accomplishing, creating, developing, or doing, is worth doing well. This negates anything that is lazy, quick, shoddy, sloppy, or mediocre. The youth are entitled to the best, but they must work for it, sacrifice for it, be patient, and do their very best at all times and in all places.

You are the master in the making, a boy, not yet transformed into a man. But what a man you will be if as a boy you master every single dream you dare to dream.

Exceptional blessings are given to those who demonstrate exceptional strength. There is an enormous difference between physical strength and spiritual strength. Here in mortality, physical strength is a raw energy and is a limited source of power. Spiritual strength, on the other hand, is eternal energy - it's an unlimited source of power.

At the end of each day ask yourself the following questions: "What have I learned today? How am I improving? What am I doing that I should not be doing? What am I not doing that I should be doing? Have I been of service to others today? Have I done my very best today to be better than I was yesterday? Am I shaping my day or is my day shaping me? Do I form habits or do habits form me? Do I learn from my mistakes and move on, or do my mistakes maim me and cripple my character? Am I taught by my trials or do my trials turn me to defeat? Have I done the very best I could, or could I possibly do any better?" Evaluate what has or has not happened at the conclusion of every day and commit to do better with each new day that comes your way.

Truthfully, the key to most success stories is stamina. Are you in it for the long haul? Ask yourself, what, if anything, will deter you from accomplishing your goals? What will keep you focused and going when the trials come and the ground beneath your feet gives way? Where's your strength? Will you be able to endure the pain for the prize? The bad times for the good times? Stamina (perseverance) and determination when combined with courage, faith, creativity, commitment, and enthusiasm will always move you forward and push you along, especially when the going gets tough. Tough times come to everyone - they always have and they always will. The test is whether or not you are ready to face those challenges. Stick with it. Stay in the game and see it through. Remember, stay focused through the game of life and you *will* win.

Improve your insight and focus on perfecting your foresight. Too many people are short-sighted because they focus on hindsight. It's easy to say what should have been done when the outcome is already known, but those who hold onto hindsight hinder their future growth. Stop looking behind you to see what you should have, would have, and could have accomplished or become. Turn around and face your future. Stay focused and you will improve your insight. Face forward and you will perfect your foresight.

The word *ability* comes from the Latin noun *habilitas*, from the adjective *habilis*, *habile*, from the verb *habere* (or habit - to have, to hold). Most people understand they must first form their habits and then their habits will form them. Our ability to do anything in life is a direct result of the habits we have formed and those we choose to create. We can create good habits and we can create bad habits. If we would like to eliminate a bad habit from our routine or lifestyle, we must replace it with a good habit - one for the other and only one at a time. Habits take time. We become more able and our capacity increases when we focus on developing good habits and replacing less desirable habits with life-changing habits.

Why do we tell on ourselves? Every little action we do gives an indication of who we are. At best or worst, our actions, and words reflect our thoughts which is a reflection of our hearts. Whether for better or for worse, we tell on ourselves. The truth is told by what we do.

We must live lives that follow "laws and rules invented by reason" (Muteferrika). If not, we will live lawless lives, and will cease to reason intelligently. A civilization is created or destroyed by the laws they observe and obey or by those to which they fail to adhere. In speaking of intelligence, laws give us freedom. They do not enslave us, they empower and enable us to be more effective and more productive. Laws and rules create order. They cooperate together and provide guide-lines by which any individual can gauge their progression. Just as there are scientific laws and rules of order, so are there spiritual laws, physical laws, financial laws, mental, emotional, and social laws. We must be law abiding citizens in each of these areas. Rules regulate our conduct and continually remind us of what is and is not correct, right, permissible, acceptable, and allowable. Commit to be and become law abiding citizens in everything you do.

Embrace *philosophia* (the word from which our modern word philosophy comes), which, literally translated, means: "The love of wisdom; to lift the soul to truth." Constantly yearn to know the truth. Seek after wisdom and love knowledge. Learn as much as you can. Never stop learning.

Any hurtful deed done angrily is always done regretfully. A meaningless act often brings remorseful resentments and all worthless acts bring disgracing defilement. Think very carefully before doing or saying anything.

Embark on a quest of knowledge. Study, learn, inquire, and continue to be curious. Curiosity increases your intensity towards increasing your intelligence. Seek, explore, and discover new knowledge on a daily basis. Determine what areas of study to focus on and expand your areas of expertise. You do not need to know everything about a particular subject (nor will you ever), but choose subjects that interest and fascinate you. Spend a lifetime learning everything you can about a particular subject or subjects. In the beginning, you are the student, but in time you may become the teacher. Share your knowledge with others. Teach them what you have learned, but never stop learning. Consciously choose to remain curious at all times and in all situations.

As a natural habit, we too often indulge ourselves in something not worth being indulged. We sometimes settle and become something less than what we could and should be. At times we become complacent and stop progressing. There is no mountain too high, no ocean too vast, and no dream too difficult or unconquerable. What we seek to accomplish everyday will stand as a constant reminder of what we can and will do if we give it our all and do our very best - every day.

Everything we do or try to do is somehow a reflection of the traditions of our ancestors. We are the product of their ingenuity. We would not be where we are today without our ancestors, so we must each learn from them.

Some people are spiritually bankrupt. Others are physically bankrupt. There are those who are emotionally bankrupt, and still others who are socially bankrupt. At times in our lives, each of us experience brief moments of personal bankruptcy. When this happens we experience spiritual, physical, emotional, and social static in our lives that creates friction, tension, and undue (and unwanted) disturbance. This becomes an annoyance to ourselves and others, and should bother us enough to motivate us into action. Sometimes before we reach the highest heights, we sink to the lowest lows and at times, get buried in the depths of discouragement. To fill our spiritual, physical, emotional, social, and financial reservoirs we must plan ahead and know where to turn in our moments of crises.

The written word and the spoken tongue are often on two very different ends of the spectrum. What one reads, one seldom speaks or can effectively or eloquently convey to another. Quite often we find that we cannot adequately express ourselves, our intents, our thoughts, or our motives. We must strive to learn more about our language and how to better verbalize our thoughts and opinions.

It has often been said that faith precedes miracles, but that statement demonstrates only half of the miraculous power of faith. Simply put, faith precedes miracles, and faith *produces* miracles.

43

Teach self-reliance. Too many people have come to expect and rely upon charity, freebies, gifts, free handouts, bonuses, and temporary government assisted programs which turn into long-term rehabilitation care and often do more damage than good. We must teach and learn the importance of work well done, an honest days work, and the personal satisfaction of doing our best at all times. Tough times fall on the majority of people at various stages in their lives. It's part of life. We all will have good days *and* bad days. That being said, each of us must make the most of our good days and prepare for times of uncertainty. We must knowingly make plans for the unknown. We must expect that bad times will come and we must be prepared. If we are prepared, we will not fear, worry, or be filled with negativity and pessimism. We will have an optimistic outlook and will know we are ready.

We all are born with many talents and gifts. The more we share these gifts the more gifts we receive. Now that is not why we share our talents and gifts with others, but it is a natural result of the gift of giving. We must share our talents and gifts with the world.

We must serve and sacrifice, selflessly doing all we can to strengthen our neighbors - to uplift and edify. We can be the means of improving others lives, lifting their spirits, strengthening them when they are weak, encouraging them when they are down on themselves and are feeling low. As we give to others what we think we cannot give or do not have, we in turn will receive from others what they thought they did not have and could not do.

Redefine your expectations of yourself and of others. Generally speaking, the expectations people set for themselves and for others are either too high or too low. Far too many individuals are too demanding of themselves, which leads to setting unrealistic goals and impossible deadlines that create expectations that can never be achieved. Unrealistic expectations can prevent you from progressing because you become very frustrated with your inability to accomplish all you wanted to accomplish when you thought you would or could. We are often too demanding of ourselves and many times too demanding of others. It's important to push and stretch ourselves, but we must not set ourselves up for failure. Realize that it's okay if we don't always accomplish everything on our checklists or to do lists. We will fall short occasionally and we won't always hit the target, but that's okay. We are not perfect nor will we ever be perfect in this life. That's okay.

You and I were born with an amazing gift. This gift gives us an unlimited capacity for power, wealth, intelligence, freedom, strength, spirituality, love, and success. Even though we have this unlimited power within our reach, we often do not realize the possibilities of this power or our own potential. This gift is desirable only if we want it. It's ours and we need this gift more than we know. Without air to breathe our lungs would collapse and we would die. Without this gift, the gift of self control, we cannot progress, improve, or accomplish all we want to accomplish. When we learn to control ourselves, our thoughts, our words, our actions, our attitudes, our desires, and our strengths and weaknesses, we improve.

45

The "scapegoat sickness" is a terrible sickness to have. When one catches it, they become immune to all of life's problems and blame everyone around them for everything. All of sudden, they are guiltless of every wrong decision they have made or past, present, and future problems they create, experience, or with which they are confronted. These are some of the symptoms of the "scapegoat sickness":

(1) It's *always* someone else's fault.
(2) Everyone is out to get me.
(3) The glass is always half full (if there actually is anything in the glass at all - most times there isn't even a glass).
(4) I will do as little as possible, and what I actually do won't be my best work anyway.
(5) Everyone else is wrong. Period. I know I'm right and I don't care what they think.

If you feel you might be coming down with the "scapegoat sickness," please seek help immediately. This sickness doesn't go away easily and often times it leads to other more deadly diseases. Take action now and get immunized against the "scapegoat sickness."

Most likely, we have heard the saying: "offense is never given, it is only taken." In all honesty, offense can be given, but it doesn't have to be taken. Don't be so easily offended by what others say and do. Others may offend, but we choose whether or not we let their comments and actions offend us. Be the bigger person.

Discover the importance of Plato's four different stages (or levels) of procedure for and toward true understanding (from The Republic):

Level 1 - *Ignorance*
Level 2 - *Opinion*
Level 3 - *Reason*
Level 4 - *Intelligence*

Never remain in ignorance. Strive to learn and grow. Having an opinion is a good start, but make sure it is an educated opinion. When you learn how to reason correctly you will understand the difference between reasoning and simply arguing. Do not argue. Seek to gain more intelligence but never claim to have acquired intelligence. The truly intelligent person never stops learning or striving for personal improvement. They also never claim or boast of being very intelligent because there is always more to learn. Strive to increase your intelligence, and use it wisely.

We cannot take ourselves too seriously. Sometimes we get caught up in our quality and quantity of life and fail to see the big picture. We try to keep pace with the sprinters and mad dashers of life but feel we are being outpaced and outrun. We tend to look to someone else's success, strengths, and accomplishments as proof that we don't measure up. We sometimes feel as if our efforts go unnoticed, unappreciated, and as a result we feel unaccepted. This is unacceptable. We must rejoice in life and bask in the sun of simplicity and the shadows of serenity.

Conquer your fears. We are all afraid of something. Most fear is unnecessary and creates worry, anxiety, trauma, and undesirable side effects resulting in poor physical, mental, emotional, spiritual, and financial health. In my opinion, there are four main levels of fear each of us must pass through and on which we must continually work and improve: (1) the fear of ridicule, (2) the fear of abandonment, (3) the fear of the unknown, and (4) the fear of not doing the right thing.

The **first fear**, the *"fear of ridicule,"* is the fear of embarrassment, worrying and focusing too much on what other people say and think about us or what we fear they might say or think about us.

The **second fear**, the *"fear of abandonment,"* is the fear that, based on our good or bad choices, we may be abandoned by our family members, friends, coworkers, and neighbors - those we trust and admire most. This fear may cause us to feel alone, unaccepted, and unwanted.

The **third fear**, the *"fear of the unknown,"* is the fear of what might be. This fear is the fear of the future, what we don't know, and haven't done before.

The **fourth fear**, the *"fear of not doing the right thing,"* is when our fear in life focuses on *not* doing what should be done. This is a good fear to have. When we reach this level, our main priority is doing what is right at all times. We no longer regard the previous three fears because our primary prerogative in life is in being honest, true, having character, and integrity. The only thing we should fear is that we are not doing our best, having character or striving to be better. We would be wise to eliminate the first three fears and embrace the fourth fear.

We don't know how much a person is appreciated until they are gone. We slip through this life as the sands of time. Slowly our years plummet toward the baron glass of our existence. Some years seem to fall quickly and others take their time. We don't realize how little time we have left. All we know is that the sands of time run dry and our lives pass on. We must do all we can to take full advantage of our lives. We must make the most of each day. Some procrastinate living because they think they have all the time in the world. This may be cliché, but we *must* live today as if it were our last. We must make the most of each minute and experience life to the fullest. Don't procrastinate living the life you want to live.

I suggest reading at least four books per month. This is what I suggest, reading-wise, to be done each month (one book per week - if possible):

Study one artist/composer/dancer/entertainer
Study one philosopher/sage/revolutionary thinker
Study one scientist/inventor/business leader, etc.
Study one prophet/apostle/religious leader

If you can read one book about each of these types of individuals, or one book covering the field, topic, or area of study of each of these every month, you will gain a greater understanding of the world around you. Enrich your life by learning and studying the lives of the greatest men and women who have lived on earth.

There are seven main periods of art: (1) **Early** (up to 1400s) which includes Gothic, Byzantine, and Ancient art, (2) **Renaissance** (1400s-1500s) which includes early Renaissance, High Renaissance, and Northern Renaissance, (in addition there are the Renaissance Classicism and Neoclassicism periods during and shortly after the Renaissance period) (3) **Baroque** (1600s-1700s) which includes Spanish, German, French, English, Dutch, Flemish, and Italian Baroque works (some of the most notable), (4) **Romanticism** (1790-1800s), (5) **Impressionism** (later 1800s) which includes Neo-Impressionist and Post-Impressionist, (6) **Modern** (late 1800s-1950s) which include Surrealism, Abstract Expressionism, Symbolism, Fauvism, Cubism, Expressionism, Dadaism, Regionalism, Muralism, Abstract, Sculpture, and (7) **Contemporary** which includes Surrealism, Minimalism, Pop Art, Installation Art, Abstract, and Sculpture.

Study and learn as much as you can about each of these art periods. Below are some of the most well known artists from these periods. Learn as much as you can about each of them and create and compile a list of your own (I've only included some of the most well known artists).

Leonardo da Vinci (Renaissance), **Raphael** (High Renaissance), **Michelangelo** (Renaissance), **Albrecht Dürer** (Northern Renaissance), **Jan Van Eyck** (Early Renaissance), **El Greco** (Spanish Renaissance), **Caravaggio** (Baroque), **Peter Paul Rubens** (Baroque), **Jan Vermeer** (Baroque), **Rembrandt** (Baroque), **Claude Monet** (Impressionism), **Pierre-Auguste Renoir** (Impressionism), **Edgar Degas** (Impressionism), **Edouard Manet** (Impressionism), **Vincent Van Gogh** (Post-Impressionism), **Pablo Picasso** (Cubism).

There are many more artists. Visit http://en.wikipedia.org/wiki/Western_painting.

There are seven main periods or eras of music: (1) **Medievel Era** (500-1400s), (2) **Renaissance Era** (1400s-1600s), (3) **Baroque Era** (1600s-1760), (4) **Classical Era** (1730-1820), (5) **Romantic Era** (1815-1910), (6) **20ᵗʰ Century Era** (1900-2000, modern period from 1890-1930, contemporary from 1975-present), and (7) The **21ˢᵗ Century Era** (2000-present).

Study and learn as much as you can about each of these music periods. Below are some of the most well known composers from these periods. Learn as much as you can about each of them and create and compile a list of your own (I've only included some of the most well known composers - I wanted to include many more).

Baroque Era (1600s-1760): Johann Pachelbel, Antonio Vivaldi, Jean-Philippe Rameau, Johann Sebastian Bach, Domenico Scarlatti, and George Frideric Handel.

Classical Era (1730-1820): Christoph Willibald Gluck, Carl Phillipp Emanuel Bach, Joseph Hayden, Wolfgang Amadeus Mozart, Ludwig van Beethoven (also in the Romantic Era), and Franz Schubert (also in the Romantic Era).

Romantic Era (1815-1910): Ludwig van Beethoven, Niccolo Paganini, Carl Maria von Weber, Carl Czerny, Gioacchino Rossini, Franz Shubert, Hector Berlioz, Johann Strauss I, Felix Mendelssohn, Frédéric Chopin, Robert Schumann (and Clara Schumann), Franz Liszt, Richard Wagner, Giuseppe Verdi, Jacques Offenbach, Johann Strauss II, Johannes Brahms, Pyotr Illyich Tchaikovsky, Antonin Dvořák, Edvard Grieg, Nikolai Rimsky-Korsakov, Giacomo Puccini, Gustav Mahler, Richard Strauss, Jean Sibelius, Alexander Scriabin, and Sergei Rachmaninoff.

20ᵗʰ/21ˢᵗ Century (1900 - present): Claude Debussy, Arnold Schoenberg, Maurice Ravel, Béla Bartōk, Igor Stravinsky, Heitor Villa-Lobos, Sergei Prokofiev, George Gershwin, Aaron Copland, Dimitri Shostakovich, and Leonard Bernstein.

There are many more composers I wish I could have listed. To learn more visit this website: http://en.wikipedia.org/wiki/List_of_classical_music_composers_by_era

If you don't attempt something you won't achieve anything. Those who never try do not succeed because they have never experienced failure. To improve and progress you must experience, at least to some degree, defeat, failure, setbacks, road blocks, trials, and problems that help you look for solutions, find answers, and adjust, re-think, re-evaluate, and redo what must be done to turn things around. You never know what you can do and what you will accomplish until you try.

The law of the harvest states we will reap what we sow. It also states we don't get something for nothing. Farmers would be unwise and foolish to plant their crop the night before the harvest is scheduled to be harvested. Likewise, if farmers plant the seeds but never weed or water their gardens, their harvest will not be worth harvesting because it will either be overrun with weeds or will be meager, insufficient, and unprofitable. Farmers religiously follow the law of harvest. They plan their schedule around the seasons and work with the weather. In our own lives, we would do well to follow the example of the farmers and realize that we are sowing thoughts of positivity and negativity on a daily basis. We are sowing optimistic outlooks and pessimistic paradigms that either convince us and compel us to do more, be more, and help others, or contort and distort our perspective of ourselves and others. Either way, we will harvest what we sow and be delighted or devastated by what we have planted and continually plant in our hearts and our thoughts.

Some people overreact. They make mountains out of mole hills. They see problems instead of solutions. They focus on the worst and don't look for the best or believe in it. The most trivial and insignificant incidents escalate and erupt into unbelievably blown out of proportion problems that did not exist in the beginning, are not (and never) necessary, and do more harm than good. More often than not, the majority of problems are produced by our negative reactions to events, situations, circumstances, incidents, and the choices and actions others make which are out of our control. We can only control ourselves and how we act and react to everything and everyone else.

Come what may and enjoy it. Too many people let the downpour of rainy days dampen their spirits. If plans don't stay on schedule or if they somehow change or fall apart altogether don't worry - ride out the storm. Dance in the rain, play in the puddles. Don't worry about getting wet, and simply enjoy the storm. Embrace the change. The storm may be unexpected and may even be unwanted, but don't ever let it be about the storm. Focus on your reaction to the turbulent times. Do you crumble when catastrophes come or do you stand strong and face the floods of change? Don't ever focus on your stormy surroundings. Instead, focus on your ability to face the flood of change. Focus on your strength to stabilize yourself and those around you during the storms of sad times. You can't predict when the storms of life will hit you, but you can prepare yourself mentally, emotionally, and spiritually to face the challenges that blow your way.

Any old fool can rattle off any regurgitated garbage, recalling what others have thought, what the wise have written, and what many have said before. But only the brave dare say what needs to be said, what must be said, and sadly, what many will never say. They tell the truth, and if they don't know the truth or don't have all the facts, they simply say, "I don't know." Too many expound on the muck and the mire, and the obscurities and the mysteries. They delve into that which cannot be explained, that which will not and may never be explained, and far too often focus too much energy on that which has no explanation or *needs* no explanation. Speak simply but with authority. Say what is true but never offend, degrade, or humiliate. Be true to your values, to your beliefs, to yourself, and to each other.

Before you speak ask yourself the following questions:

What am I going to say?
Why do I *feel* I need to say it?
How am I going to say it?
Will what I say help or hurt this person?
Will what I say uplift and edify or degrade and defile?
Am I only concerned with my own best interests or am I thinking of others and putting their needs above my own?
Would I and those around me be better off if I refrained from speaking altogether?

Even constructive criticism is still destructive. It tears down in an effort to teach. Instead build others up. Find ways to correct and perfect but kindly object and never reject.

Happiness is the essence of *being*. Being happy is the art of knowing that you, and you alone, are responsible for your attitude. You can consciously choose to embrace enthusiasm, to always operate with an optimistic outlook, and to smile and enjoy every good and bad experience in life. No one can *make* you unhappy. No one can *force* you to frown, dampen your day, or strip you of your self-image or self-respect. They may tempt you to think terrible thoughts or threaten you with tyrannical deeds, but *you* are in charge of yourself and your *own* happiness. Happiness is an inside job. It must come from within and should not be dependent on other individuals, outside influences, circumstances or situations. You, and you alone, are the guardian of your gift of happiness. Regardless of what happens in your life, what successes or failures you experience, you may choose to walk with happiness or shuffle about in sadness. The choice is yours, and yours alone.

Create your own think tank. The greatest computer ever created is the one inside your cranium. Your thoughts can be brought to life. Embrace creativity and let the little abstract abnormalities of your thoughts mesh and mold together. It doesn't matter whether you think slowly or quickly - what matters is that you think. Think tanks were created to let brilliant thinkers think thoughts they've never thought before. Surround yourself with many who think as you do and even more with those who think differently than you. You must think creatively *and* effectively. Actualize your thoughts and create your world anew.

What do you see when you look in the mirror? Do you see your strengths or your weaknesses? Your successes or your failures? Your potential or your limitations? Each of us has had varying experiences, some positive and others negative. Some have been to our benefit and others, sadly, to our detriment. Some of us have been inspired and encouraged by others. Some of us have not. We each have moments where we get down on ourselves and chide ourselves for not doing our best, being better, knowing more, doing more, accomplishing more, earning more, etc. The list goes on and on. We sometimes feel the need to be everything to everyone - to be able to do everything and to do it well. But we do not. There are days when it *is* in our best interest to relax, take it easy, and do absolutely nothing. And that is wonderful! We need days and sometimes weeks like this. It helps us re-ignite our energies and better focus our attention on the fact that we are human. We are not super-human, no matter how hard we try or pretend to be. We cannot do everything all of the time and we all need "lazy days" where we enjoy doing nothing or very little of it. We can't do this all of the time, nor would we truthfully want to, but we can pause, and even stop occasionally, to gear up for the non-stop - on the go, hustle bustle of living that we experience every day. Instead of getting down on yourself when you're having a "down" moment, give yourself some leisure time and go easy on your perceived reflection of what may or may not be happening. You are doing the very best you can. You are giving so much and helping so many. You deserve a few moments, every now and then, to yourself. By doing this, you will be better energized to give life your all when you have taken the necessary "time-out" you need to get you back in the game of life. Don't get down on yourself, take a break and relax. You deserve it and you have earned it!

Be prepared. Scouts have this phrase memorized. It's their motto. But what does it really mean to *be* prepared? Preparations must be made but they cannot be made hastily. It often takes weeks, months, years, and even a lifetime to fully understand and actualize what it means to truly *be* prepared. Generally speaking, we find out how unprepared we are when the unexpected happens. Calamities, disease, acts of God, and other such unknowns are always lurking, and we must be prepared for them. We must be ready. But we must think about preventative preparation, spiritual preparation, mental preparation, financial preparation, structural preparation, and family preparedness. What are we doing to improve and strengthen our situation spiritually, mentally, financially, structurally, and individually and collectively as a family, a community, a state, territory, nation, and ultimately as a world wide effort to be ready for the unknown, the unexpected, and very often the unwanted? Are we prepared? Are we ready in all areas and in all aspects of our life? We must continually remind ourselves to be preparing and to be prepared. Anything can happen to anyone at any given time. Expect the unexpected. BE PREPARED!

If you try to rationalize what you did or did not do based on what you do or do not know, you protect yourself with ignorance and shun true intelligence. Your actions are then mockery because if you do not know why you have done something - you cannot receive the benefit of having done it. Always think before doing anything, but find purpose in everything you do.

Each book I read becomes a conversant friend with whom I travel and experience life and from whom I gain a greater appreciation of diversity, philosophy, history, world cultures, religious creeds, human superiority and inferiority, and the joys and sorrows of all mankind. I gain a new perspective, renewed hope, spiritual enlightenment, and a greater understanding of my surroundings, of my neighbors, my friends, my family, and myself.

Life is a string of pearls and problems. Some would have you look for the silver lining, others might tell you to buck up - that the buck stops here and that we are the keepers of our treasured keepsakes: time, freedom, faith, love, choice and accountability, and are able and capable of creating our own future. Both are correct. Both see possibility and responsibility. Both respect creativity and productivity. Both want the best out of life and are willing to stand up for what they believe. Both, undoubtedly, know there are good times and bad times and that both are essential for our well being in life. Accept that you will have problems and difficulties with each day, but don't think that the problems are bad in any way. Problems simply need solutions. Problems will not prevent you from progressing. They simply require a little more time and thought - focus, and preparation. If you prepare yourself for the fact that you may encounter many problems each week or day, you will better understand how problems become powerful teaching examples that strengthen us and help polish and refine us. In many ways, the problems help us become more like the pearl - polished and refined from year to year until eventually, the pearl grows in size and worth while becoming more and more beautiful all the while.

People are the problem, but people are also the solution. You can look at anyone and pick apart their strengths and weaknesses. You can blame others and label them as problematic, closed-minded, different, indifferent, uncooperative, unproductive, and incapable of much, or you can view them as problem-solvers, open-minded, maybe peculiar - but no different than any of us, completely cooperative and obliging - even at times over zealous to accommodate and please our stubbornness, very productive and actively engaged in doing good works, and more than capable of doing anything they put their minds to or attempt to do. You see, many times, the people who are the problem stare us in the face every time we look into a mirror and the people who have endless solutions and profound assistance to and for us are those around us who live the same hustle and bustle life we do. We all share common ground and choose whether we will be the problem or the solution each and every day. Don't create unnecessary problems. Bring out the problem-solvers in everyone you meet. Be part of the solution, but never be a problem for others or yourself.

I believe we must not place as much emphasis on *what* we will do or be when we grow up, graduate from school, or set out to make our way in the world, but rather, place more emphasis on *who* we will be and more important who we would like to become. Yes, we must focus on skills, aptitude, abilities, knowledge, etc., but we must consider character, values, beliefs, ideals, morals, and self worth in addition to, if not more important than, skills, ability, and knowledge. To *know* is good, to *do* is better, to *be* is best. We must focus on being and becoming.

59

Life is one well-written parable. There are many morals and lessons to be learned from day to day life experiences - both the good and the bad, the positive and the negative, the just and the unjust, the humorous and the sad. Life is a roller coaster ride and we each have our ups *and* downs.

- Jerald Simon

Parables

(short stories and poems I have written to help
teach values and principles about life)

Letting Go

An eaglet was learning to fly with his mother eagle. She was a proud new mother and this was her first eaglet. The mother flew higher and higher and then turned upside down and dropped the eaglet. The eaglet flapped his little wings as fast as he could, but he continued to fall. The nervous mother quickly swooped down to catch the frightened eaglet. This went on for quite some time until another eagle stopped the mother.

"Mother eagle," said the more experienced eagle, "you are not letting your eagle *really* fall. He cannot fly until he learns what it feels like to fall on his own. You are catching him too early. Let him fall a greater distance before you catch him. If you do this a few times you will not need to catch him because he will not rely on you. He knows you will catch him when he falls. Knowing this, your eaglet will never fly. He must think you are really letting him fall. When that happens he will stop depending on you and will learn to fly on his own."

The mother eagle followed the other eagle's wise counsel and in no time the eaglet was flying as true eagles do.

The Busy Bee

A bee was very busy pollinating flowers when a butterfly asked if it could play. One of the butterfly's favorite things to do was to dance on pretty flowers. He told the bee not to work so hard, to enjoy the flowers, and to have more fun. The bee simply said, "If I don't finish my work, you won't have any more of these pretty flowers."

Abram and Nathaniel

Many years ago there were two masters who were close friends. Both had 50 slaves. One master, Nathaniel, was ruthless and mercilessly beat and abused his slaves. They were chained, whipped, and deprived of food. He did not care about his slaves because he viewed them as slaves and not as people. He had slaves of every color and race.

The other master, Abram, was a kind and gentle man. He gave his slaves more than enough food and water. They didn't even look like slaves. He never referred to them as such, but as his friends who served and lived with his family. Not only were they cared for, but they were taught and schooled. Abram thought it wise to educate and help his fellow servants. He never beat them. He never even raised his voice. It was not necessary. Every servant worked as hard as they could because they respected their master and trusted him. He was a good man and they knew it, and everyone else knew it.

One day Nathaniel visited his friend Abram. When he arrived he could not believe how productive and prosperous his friend had become. Everything was immaculate and well kept. He had never seen so many crops. He heard the servants singing and laughing while working in the fields. His own slaves never sang. Nathaniel ran to find Abram in the house sitting down to an early lunch. Abram saluted his neighbor, thanked him for coming and asked him to stay for lunch. Nathaniel readily agreed and then asked, "Who is keeping an eye on your slaves while you lunch?"

"They are watching out for themselves," Abram replied. "They're not slaves - they're wonderful workers. I have no need to chain them up. They won't run away. We are friends. I trust them and they trust me."

Nathaniel was perplexed. "Do you mean to tell me they work without any supervision?" Abram shook his head. "They supervise their own work. I just compliment them on a job well done and praise them for their good labor. They are dedicated workers. They don't have to be told what to do. They just do it because it needs to be done. You should eliminate the word slave from your vocabulary and try to treat them as servants who help, not slaves to be used and abused. Nathaniel, you must serve those who serve you." Upon hearing this final remark Nathaniel had a change of heart. He rushed home excited to implement what he had heard.

Sadly, Nathaniel never did change. Shortly after he arrived back home an unexpected uproar began amongst his slaves. A few of them were caught trying to escape. Nathaniel's anger flared and he whipped them as he usually did. A few retaliated against Nathaniel. More slaves joined in and soon the mob of angered slaves attacked the abusive master and sent him to his death.

When Abram learned of his friend's death, he was deeply saddened. If his friend had learned to be kind and served those who served him, he would have lived a wonderfully prosperous life. How different it could have been. He might have helped others and been of service, but instead he chose to enslave and torture mankind and paid the sad price by losing his life.

Something Shiny

A young man went searching for diamonds. He had heard of diamonds, but had never seen them before. He didn't know what they looked like or where to find them, but he knew they were very valuable. He set off on a journey to find them. His father told him it would be advantageous for the son to see what diamonds looked like before searching for them. The son left hastily without heeding the advice of his father.

After spending years searching for them in vain, the son returned home and confessed to his father that he was a failure. His father asked if he had found anything of interest over the years. The young man bowed his head in shame and admitted that all he had found was nothing more than a handful of stones. He said as he was riding a camel in Africa something shimmery had caught his eye and he had gathered up a handful of these pretty, shiny rocks.

His father immediately realized what the shiny stones were and told his son he'd found diamonds! The son frowned. He had seen *thousands* of those rough, but unpolished pretty stones along the way but didn't pick them up. He marveled at how they glistened in the sunlight, and thought they looked lovely, but he didn't know they were diamonds. Had he known the worth of these shiny stones and what to look for before his journey, he could have come home with thousands or even tens of thousands of beautiful, priceless diamonds. Years had been wasted. He often lamented, "If only I had known what to look for before setting out on my journey. If only I had listened to my father's counsel before I left home - I could have returned having been obedient."

The Sloppy Sloth from Slothville

Deep in the tropical rain forest there lived an unhappy sloth named Slog. Slog was a very sloppy sloth. He was dirty, smelly, and no one wanted to be around Slog because he was a slob. In addition, Slog was very lazy and slow. It took him a long time to do anything. Sadly, Slog never changed. No one ever came to visit him. His friends stopped trying to help him because he wouldn't help himself. He became known as "The Sloppy Slog from Slothville." No one likes a slob.

Contented

A man was once very content to live a simple life. When asked by his family, friends, and neighbors, why he lived so simply, he said, "I don't need much to make me happy as long as my family, friends, and neighbors are happy. *That* is all I need and want in life." This man lived a long, wonderful, and happy life. He lived simply, but fully. He gave generously and completely, without any thought of receiving anything in return. Strangers praised his name. Neighbors, friends, and family members revered him, but he only thought of them - of their wants and needs. He never spoke of himself or his difficulties. In fact, he never really spoke to others of their difficulties either. He praised others and complimented them. He always had a smile on his face and a wonderful, warm embrace for everyone. He was father to everyone. He listened intently to others when they spoke and gave wise words of wisdom to them if they asked for advice. When he died, everyone mourned. He was loved by all and everyone lived better lives because of him. He lived simply and he simply was - a father and friend to all.

Thank You

Everything had fallen apart in Daniel's life. There seemed to be nothing left for him. He thought his life was ruined and felt as though he had nothing to live for. Daniel had hit rock bottom and wanted to end everything.

Daniel had been one of the top executives in his organization. Graduating at the top of his class had taken some work, but it was nothing when compared with how quickly he had risen within the company to become second in command. He always spoke with a smile and had a twinkle in his eye that caught others off guard and kept a person riveted. His positive personality and charismatic character brought so much hope to the other employees in his organization that people depended on him. He was beloved by all and had been the center of attention for quite some time. All eyes were on him because he was next in line to become the CEO. At age 36, Daniel would be the youngest president this company had ever had.

Everything seemed perfect, but that's when the black envelope arrived. Daniel had been on a business trip, meeting with other employees in other states. When he returned home, there was a stack of mail that had been piling up in his mailbox. He expected the usual bills, junk mail, and family letters, but there was a black envelope with an inscription: "To Mr. Daniel - The most worthless man on earth. You deserve what you get."

Upon opening the envelope, Daniel pulled out a hand-written letter that spoke of all of Daniel's shortcomings. The letter went into great detail about his mistakes and failures with the company, and even pointed out problems in his personal life. The letter was written with hatred and vengeance. There was no signature and no return address. At that moment, Daniel felt as if he truly were the most worthless man on earth.

Every week a new black envelope appeared in his mail box. Each new letter was worse than the previous ones. Days and weeks went by and Daniel continued to sink into a self-made pit of despair. He stopped taking care of his appearance. Things began to slip through the cracks. He became more irritated and frustrated with others. His anger raged and his temper became unbearable. Daniel looked at others with hatred, fear, and jealousy. He began to lose interest in life. The arguments between him and his wife reached an all time high and his wife moved out. Not only had Daniel's work capacity decreased, but his attitude became bitter and his positive personality was so poisoned by pessimism, that people began to avoid him altogether. No one could depend on him and frankly, no one wanted to be around him.

As Daniel was getting ready for work one morning, there was a knock on the door. His wife's attorney was delivering divorce papers. When Daniel arrived at work he was told to meet with the president of the company. Daniel knew his performance and productivity with the company had declined, but the president told Daniel that he had one day to remove all of his personal items from his office. Daniel was fired because he was bringing the company morale down and affecting customer relations with the company and their customers, due to his negative attitude and outlook on life.

Everything had ended. He gathered his belongings and drove away, his entire life destroyed. When he arrived home, his mailbox was full of letters he had ignored from the previous weeks. He angrily stuffed the unwanted envelopes into his dirty coat pocket and began to walk slowly down the lonely street where he had once been so happy.

It began to rain and his dampened spirits sank further, as if the storm within had propelled the storm about him. He passed an old abandoned building and then, as if realizing he had nothing to live for, he walked toward the decrepit edifice and scaled the winding stairs to the top. The building had been condemned one week earlier and for the first time, Daniel felt at home, as if he belonged in the condemned building.

One side of the building had been knocked down, leaving it open and uncovered. Daniel walked to the edge of the tenth floor hall where a wall had once been and looked at the ground below, feeling he was the most worthless man alive. He needed a moment to accept his fate as he embraced the realization that he had nothing to live for and was better off dead. The rain turned to hail as he was preparing to jump.

As he was about to end his life his quivering hands were fidgeting, fumbling, and trembling. He placed his hands into his wet, dirty trench coat and felt the envelopes in his pocket. As if without thinking, he pulled one letter out from the pile and decided to read it.

Daniel opened the envelope and began to read. He couldn't believe what he was reading, and as he read the letter, tears fell from his eyes -

"Daniel, you don't personally know me, but I have always looked up to you and have tried to be the kind of person you are. You are so talented and so intelligent and I have been so amazed with your accomplishments in life. I am your younger brother's age and have never had any siblings of my own. My parents were both killed in a car accident when I was in high school, so I have been alone for most of my life. I've always admired you and tried to pattern my own life after yours because of the wonderful person you are. You have been such an example to me and I want to thank you for being the kind of person I want to be. I recently finished my schooling, have started my career, and wondered if you would mentor me and help me be and become a better person. I know how optimistic and positive you are and I respect you so much. I am at a crossroads in my life right now and knew I could turn to you for help. I didn't know where else to go, but I knew if anyone could help me, you could. Thank you again for your wonderful example throughout my life. I have looked up to you as a big brother and as a father figure and am so grateful for the man you are and the man I hope to become. Please let me know if you would be willing to mentor me. I appreciate you taking the time to read this letter. Thank you so much."

Daniel stepped away from the edge and knew he had something to live for. He now knew the kind of man he needed to be and would again become. He vowed then and there to never lose sight of who he was and how he should live his life. He had lost his life because of one letter, but had gained a new life because of another.

The Fearless Frog

Once upon a time, there lived a fearless frog named Freddie. He wasn't afraid of anything. One day the other frogs dared Freddie to jump off the biggest rock into the pond. Freddie agreed to do it because he wasn't afraid of anything, or at least, he didn't want any of the other frogs to think he was. He climbed on top of the biggest rock and leapt into the air. Freddie fell and hit a rock. He broke his leg. From then on, no frogs jumped off big rocks.

A Parable of Get Rich Quick Schemes

Ralph was an intelligent man who had acquired a small fortune through his diligence, frugality, and dedication to his work. But over the years, he grew lazy and became increasingly dissatisfied with work in general. He thought of a plan to persuade others to do his work for him so he wouldn't have to do it himself.

Ralph decided to purchase a small plot of land on which to plant trees with his fortune. Having spent all he had on the land, Ralph could not afford to hire anyone to work in his fields. "I could promise people abundant wealth to buy whatever they want," he thought. "People are always on the lookout and continually looking for something for nothing. If I promise them huge returns, they'll do what I ask." With that thought, he devised his plan.

Ralph would promise each individual a continuous three dollars per day for every 10 men or women they signed up to work in his fields. Each of those 10 men could then sign up more workers and each would be guaranteed the same amount. The more people each man and woman signed up, the more money they would receive. Ralph began persuading the people by promising them easy, abundant wealth, power, and freedom to go where they wanted and to do what they pleased. He promised them they would be paid for the men and women they personally signed up and a small percentage of the amount given to every man and woman who in turn signed up or enlisted others to work in the fields as well.

Within weeks hundreds of men and women began working for Ralph. Many quit their good paying jobs, and began dreaming of fortunes, fame, and quickly becoming successful in the eyes of their peers. They all wanted a quick, easy way to wealth.

Several years passed and Ralph had become one of the wealthiest men in all the land. Thousands and tens of thousands of money hungry fortune seekers had flocked to his fields.

One bright young man was amazed at how many men and women worked for Ralph. He also noticed how poor they all were. Despite their many years of working in the fields for Ralph and recruiting more workers, they all, for the most part, remained in poverty. It seemed as if no one made any real money except for Ralph. The young man decided to confront Ralph and ask him why this was.

"Ralph," the young man began, "My name is Tom. I do not work for you, but many of my friends and family members do." Ralph looked at Tom and could tell right away he was a bright, innovative young man.

"Tom," Ralph replied, "would you like to work for me as well? With your enthusiasm and personality, I know you would make a fortune and become very wealthy. What do you say, Tom? Will you work for me and make quick, easy, money? What do you say to that, Tom?"

"No Sir," Tom stated authoritatively, "I want to own my own businesses one day. I'm impressed with what you have done in your business, but I am confused by your business model. You promise money to employees when they sign up friends and family members as additional employees. They in turn are promised money when they sign up others. But, I only see you becoming wealthy. Why doesn't anyone else make a great deal of money and become wealthy like you promised?"

Ralph could tell Tom was too smart to be lied to, so he decided to tell him the truth. "Tom, if people want something badly enough, they will work for it and get it. They must be willing to make sacrifices, but they must work for themselves. You see, as long as you work for someone else you will always be an employee. I have told the workers who work for me that they are their own bosses. They can work as much or as little as they want. I tell them their success will be based on their hard work and sacrifice, but they are still working for me and not for themselves. You see, they do not create anything, and as a result they do not own anything. I promise them more wealth if they sign up more of their friends and family members to work with them. In reality, I get cheap labor. They work for me. I'm not really working for them. I never have been. I can promise whatever I want and if they don't achieve it I blame them, telling them they need to work more, sign up more friends and family members, which they do, assuming they will make more money because they are working more."

"But they don't and never will," Tom quickly interjected disapprovingly.

"But I do, Tom. You see several of the people they sign up quit because they realize they won't make any real money working for me. You only make substantial money when you work for yourself."

"But, why would others continue to work for you when they're not making any real money doing it? Several people have left good paying jobs, security, and stability, to work for you in your fields because they think they will make a lot of money doing it. They make less now than they ever have before."

"Tom, they think they will make money instantly, and some do for a short while. They are hungry for wealth and many go from one money making idea and scheme to the next. If it doesn't produce instant results they look somewhere else for the next big money-making idea. They're greedy for money and think money grows on trees. The problem is they don't want to save up the money to buy the land where they can plant trees of their own. They don't know how to cultivate and prepare the land so the trees will grow. They don't have the patience to plant the baby trees or seedling and help them grow. They want someone else to prepare the land. They want someone else to plant the trees and take care of the trees until they grow enough to produce profitable fruit. Unfortunately, they think they can come in and pick the fruit from my trees and make a huge profit. They don't understand that they don't own the fruit. They don't own the trees, the land, or even the rights to share in the profits because all they have done is harvest the fruit. They tell their friends they can become wealthy picking the fruit. They see the profit of the fruit but don't realize the real profit and wealth lies in the land and the trees that produce the fruit, not in the fruit itself. They simply don't understand how financial success is earned through sacrifice, sweat, hard work, and ownership. They don't own anything and think they deserve to receive the real profits as a result."

Tom was amazed at the truth of Ralph's business model. Ralph used people and their weaknesses to get what he wanted. He wasn't concerned with what they wanted and what they dreamed of having. The workers in his field were only the means to an end.

"Ralph," Tom began, "Don't you feel terrible doing what you're doing? You are promising people they will have something you and I know very well they never will have if they continue to work for you."

"Tom, people will believe anything you tell them. Remember, people, for the most part, are lazy creatures and the majority of people would never take the risk of buying their own piece of land. They don't know what will happen and as a result think it is more risky working on their own for themselves, in that sense, than it is working for me or for anyone else. They feel burdened by their current positions, jobs of employment, and chosen vocations and careers. They think I am the solution to their problems. They think if they work hard enough and long enough for a short period of time they will not need to work anymore. You see Tom, successful businesses and successful people never quit working. They give 110 percent in everything they do day in and day out throughout their lives."

"Success is not necessarily measured by wealth. The people who work for others think it is, but those who do what they love doing and truly enjoy the work they do are successful. They have found their purpose in life. The people who want to make easy money and quickly rise to fame and fortune think *that* is their purpose. In the end they have no purpose because they have no direction. They want what everyone else has, but they don't want to work for it. They want an easy way to everything. They will not succeed because they don't believe in themselves and their ability to create and produce. They think there is a get rich quick program, business, venture, idea, or product that will launch them into the spotlight of success. They don't realize that the only ones who prosper from these schemes are the ones at the top. The men and women who begin these businesses know other people will fall into their traps and they do it because they are lazy."

"Tom, I worked for years and years. I know what it takes to be successful. I made a small fortune, but I lost my zeal for work. I didn't enjoy what I did. I became lazy and wanted an easy way to even more wealth. I know there is no easy way to wealth, but I knew if I convinced others there was, they would do my work for me. That bought me time to do what I wanted to while others did my work for me. The more people who work for me will help me continue to do what I love. The majority of people working for me will need to work for the rest of their lives. I didn't want that. I wanted the freedom of doing what I wanted while others did what needed to be done to sustain my lifestyle."

Tom was shocked. He couldn't believe what he was hearing. Ralph knew he was ruining the lives of the individuals who worked for him and he didn't care. He saw them as a means to an end.

"Ralph," Tom began, "thank you for explaining your get rich quick scheme. I knew I never wanted to work for a company like yours or someone like you, but I understand why you do what you do. Sadly, I understand why many people fall for it. They are being lazy and want to receive something for nothing. With a work ethic like that they never will succeed. People who continue to work for you and others like you will never succeed because they enslave themselves to your dreams, your wealth, and your success. Thank you again for explaining what you do. It has been very enlightening."

"Tom," Ralph replied, "What type of business do you want to create in the future anyway?"

"I want to create a service business called 'Success Begins with Me'. My business is designed to teach people how to start their own businesses. I want to walk them through models of successful businesses that have become successful through hard work, sacrifice, and patiently giving 110 percent in everything they do, day in and day out. My business will teach them how to be successful through workshops, seminars, and practical step by step application of hard work."

"I will invest in the dreams others have and will help

them become successful by doing what they want to do with their time and making it profitable so they can own their own land, plant their own seeds of success and reap the rewards of their own efforts. In return I will receive a small percentage of their profits as a return of my investment in helping them become successful on their own - working for themselves and creating products of their own. They will cultivate the fruit and when they pick their fruit they will be profitable because it is theirs. I will help them get started and keep them motivated to work through the difficult times, which will come, but they will succeed because they have a purpose in life. I want to help them understand which direction leads to success and which direction leads to failure. When they know and understand what they can personally do to invest in themselves and how they can work for themselves, they will enjoy the work they do and take pride in their accomplishments."

"Ralph, I want to help people learn to avoid people like you. I want them to trust their own ideas, create their own products, invest in their own talents and make their dreams become a reality because I believe in them. I believe they can and will be successful if they are shown how to be successful. Remember, you said success is not necessarily measured by wealth. As long as people continue to do what others tell them to do and believe what others tell them to believe, they will not be successful. I believe they can learn to trust their own ideas, to believe what they tell themselves to believe, and accomplish what they want to accomplish on their own. I believe that everyone can and should believe success begins with me, and I believe everyone deserves the chance to begin a new life where they are very successful in everything they do because they work for themselves.

They know where they are going and what they want to do with their lives. I believe in people and the possibility of dreams."

In Search of a Smile

Samuel grew up in a gloomy village rightly called Gloomsville. The village was founded by Gompert Gloomburg. Gompert was a grumpy old man who despised happiness, laughter, excitement, positivity, and most of all, smiling. As a young man Gompert set out to create a town where everyone could be as miserable as he was. He felt so awkward with people who laughed, smiled, and enjoyed life - primarily because he did not. Since he founded the sad little village, he only allowed sad, grumpy, miserable people to live there. Unfortunately, the idea of an entire town full of grumpy people was very appealing to many, far too many. In the beginning, hundreds of angry, frustrated people flocked to the growing village, eagerly hoping to contribute to the little village by complaining, gossiping, and spreading gloom with the other gloomy villagers who felt as bitter as they did. They felt life was unfair and that they had been treated unfairly.

Samuel's father, Sebastian, had grown up in gloomsville as a child, but left the village as a young man. Throughout his childhood, Sebastian had been very unhappy and desperately wanted to find happiness. After leaving the village, he met a sweet and beautiful girl named Sophia, whom he later married. Sebastian and Sophia were very happy about life. Sebastian had a good job, good health, and a wonderful wife. Everything was picture perfect.

A few years after their marriage, Sophia gave birth to a healthy, smiling little boy. They decided to name him Samuel. His nickname was "Samuel the smiling boy" because he always smiled. Sebastian, Sophia, and Samuel always had so much fun together as a family. They laughed together everyday. They enjoyed reading books together, playing games, walking, singing, enjoying their journey through life together. Their home was filled with happiness. Everyone smiled, for there was much to smile about. Samuel had the happiest childhood any child could ask for. His parents loved him very much, and they loved each other. Their home was filled with love, happiness, laughter, acceptance, positivity, and people who optimistically awaited the arrival of each new day - for each day was a blessing and a gift of life.

Then, when Samuel was about 8 years old everything changed. Samuel's father, Sebastian, lost his job. The family had no way of bringing in any income. There was little or no food for the family to eat because there was no way to pay for the food. Since the family had no income they could not afford to pay for their home and soon lost their home. The family stopped laughing together, for they assumed there was no reason to laugh. The family never played games with each other anymore, never read books together, sang or even enjoyed being together. They were completely miserable. Their home was filled with anger, hostility, and unkindness. Since Sebastian had lost his job, he felt worthless as a husband and as a father. He tried to get another job elsewhere, but quickly gave up. He thought he was a failure. He believed it so much that he began to fail at everything he tried. He became the failure he thought everyone else thought he was.

Sophia had also completely changed. She used to sing and whistle as she walked. Now she hung her weary head and sighed everywhere she went. Life was a burden, whereas before it had been a blessing. She never smiled. She stopped taking care of her appearance, her health declined, and she stopped trying to do anything for anyone including herself. She never had anything nice to say about anyone anymore either. She began to complain about everything to everyone. She enjoyed gossiping about others, speaking ill about them and their weaknesses behind their backs, and telling others what they didn't know, couldn't do, and would not become. She spoke so negatively about her husband and his inability to provide for their family that she and Sebastian could barely stand to be in each other's presence.

The father decided happiness did not exist. He came to the conclusion that happy people, positive, optimistic, smiling people were deluded, deranged, and living in a fairy-tale. He knew fairy-tales did not exist and remembered his sad childhood in Gloomsville. His own parents had moved to Gloomsville because they said it was where real people lived in the real world. Sebastian decided to move his sad little family to Gloomsville where they could live life as it was meant to be lived - in sadness, frustration, and negativity.

The change of scenery had been a difficult one for Samuel. Since he was only a little boy, he didn't understand why they had to move to such a place. He tried making friends with the other little children, but they were all mean. No one ever wanted to play games. All they did was make fun of one another and belittle each other. Every boy and girl failed in everything they did, in part because all they ever heard from their parents, their siblings, their neighbors, and other children their age was that they couldn't do anything. Others believed they couldn't which eventually convinced them they shouldn't. It was a terrible place.

Samuel did not fit in. At the age of 13, while walking down the dirty streets of Gloomsville, the other children were making fun of each other when a terrible fight began. A big bully pushed down a dirty little boy and made fun of him in front of everyone. All the other children laughed at the dirty little boy and told him he was stupid, ugly, and unwanted. Samuel knelt down and held out his hand to help the little boy stand up, but the little boy shook his head from side to side.

"I don't need your help," scowled the little boy at Samuel. "I don't need anyone's help at all. Get away from me you freak!"

Samuel was hurt. All he wanted to do was help the boy, but no one in Gloomsville ever accepted help, in part, because few ever offered to help. Samuel felt so alone. At night he would lay awake in his bed and remember the songs he used to sing with his family. He remembered the games they played, the walks they would take, and the times they burst into laughter for no particular reason at all. How happy his memories were. The reality of his situation would return as he heard his parents yelling and screaming at each other below. How awful his life had become.

Why, he silently wondered, did people resign themselves to resentment, to ridicule, and to rage? "How," he thought out loud to himself, "could people be content to live each day in misery, without smiling, laughing, singing, and enjoying life?" Samuel knew there must be more to life than negativity, loneliness, and sadness.

Years went by and Samuel grew up. The sad mean

little children turned into sad, mean adults. They complained about everything. No one ever had anything nice to say about anyone - especially Samuel.

Everyone made fun of Samuel - children, teenagers, and adults. He had become the village outcast. They referred to him in mockery as "Samuel the Saint," or "Sammy Sunshine" and other names referring to his optimistic attitude. Despite the gloom, the misery, and the pollution of pessimism, Samuel had remained positive, happy, and upbeat in spite of everything.

He had lived so long in Gloomsville that happiness, singing, laughter, and smiling faces were only images in his memory. He had never experienced anything positive while living in the gloomy village and often thought he had dreamed up the positive experiences of his childhood.

Finally, at the age of 20, Samuel grew tired of Gloomsville. Being old enough, he informed his parents that he was going to leave Gloomsville once and for all. They, of course, discouraged him, telling him he was a dreamer hoping for a fairy-tale. They told him to accept the world as it was and be realistic about what life was and was not supposed to be like.

Samuel thanked them for their concern, but said it was his life and he wanted to be happy. He wanted to enjoy life. He longed to sing, and dance, and smile.

"Samuel, I left Gloomsville once hoping to change the world, but the real world will never change," Sebastian sneered. "You think life is filled with happy optimistic people, don't you? You honestly think people are positive and that people can avoid being negative, pessimistic, or unhappy, don't you? You'll be very surprised once you discover as I did that people are sad, miserable souls. They want to be sad because it makes them feel good.

They enjoy complaining because it helps them feel justified for thinking negatively. People want to be miserable because it gives them the opportunity to make excuses. If things don't turn out the way they've planned they can complain and blame everyone else. It *is* who we are. It is what we do and the sooner you learn that the better."

The room fell silent as Samuel stared at his angry father and mother. He once looked up to them, but now realized they enjoyed being miserable and didn't want others to be happy. Samuel came to the conclusion that the inhabitants of Gloomsville didn't want to see anyone, including themselves, succeed or be happy. Misery loves company. They actually delighted and enjoyed being miserable together, but didn't enjoy their own misery unless their neighbors and other family members were as miserable, if not more so, than they were.

"Father, I'm leaving Gloomsville," pronounced Samuel defiantly, and with that he gathered up his things and left the gloomy village.

Samuel was in search of a smile. He knew it existed. He had seen it as a child and saw it every time he closed his eyes. His memory would not let him forget how wonderful a smile looked, but more important, how wonderful it made him feel when he saw someone smile or when he had smiled as a child.

After traveling for days Samuel came to a small town nestled between two large mountains. A group of people lived in the town between the two mountains, but they were very peculiar. These people were not angry or miserable at all, but he knew they were not happy, positive, or excited about life either. As Samuel met these people they did not frown, gossip, or make fun of one another, but they did not say anything positive or encouraging about each other or smile either.

"What is this town?," Samuel curiously asked one of the townspeople on the street.

"What do you mean young man?" A little old man responded unsurely.

"You see," Samuel began, "I came from a village of grumpy, miserable people, but when I was a little boy I lived in a very happy place where everyone was nice, and positive. There was singing and dancing, and smiling. Does any of that happen in this town?"

"No my boy," whispered the quaint little old man. "This is the Town of Indifference. There is no misery or anger here, but there is no laughter, singing, or smiling either."

"May I ask why not?" Samuel was puzzled and wondered what kind of town this was.

"Well young man, people don't have anything to complain about, but they don't have anything so smile about either. We're indifferent," he said matter-of-factly.

"Is there anyone who would know how I could find the village where I had been so happy as a child?" Samuel looked into the old man's eyes, almost pleading to know if he knew something - anything.

"My young friend, if you would like, you may climb the mountain and speak with the old sage. I hear he is a wise old hermit who lives on top of one of the mountain peaks. He has lived a long time and experienced a great deal. People come from far and wide to speak with him and ask him questions pertaining to life. Because of his experience, he can relate with people from all walks of life."

"How will I find the old sage on top of the mountain? What do I do when I meet him?"

84

"You'll know my boy. The questions will come to you as will the answers."

And with that the old man walked away. Samuel was left to himself. Samuel decided to follow the old man's advice and climb to the mountain top.

Samuel climbed the first peak and looked out at the valley on the side. He saw Gloomsville. He watched as people busily scampered up and down the streets. They seemed so normal from a distance, but Samuel knew they were miserably scurrying along making fun of one another as they went their way. He watched for a time and felt so grateful to be standing on the peak far away from Gloomsville.

Samuel descended the first peak and began ascending the second peak after realizing the wise old sage wasn't on the first peak. When he made it to the top of the second peak, he rested and looked out over this new valley on the opposite side. No one lived in this valley. It was beautiful with trees, flowers, rivers, and lakes. Samuel had never seen anything so beautiful.

A few feet below the mountain peak was a little shack. After knocking on the door and waiting for a few moments, Samuel went to the back of the shack. Out back there was a little trail, well beaten and often used. Samuel followed the trail for a few feet. Suddenly he stopped. Someone was following him. Slowly turning around, while cautiously looking over his broad shoulder and crouching a little, he noticed an older gentleman resting against a big evergreen tree.

"Are you the wise old sage I've heard about?" Samuel looked at the tired gentleman as he caught his breath.

"I don't know how wise I am, but I do feel old - and getting older by the minute. You must be Samuel." The old sage pursed his lips together and cocked his gray head as if to look heavenward.

"How do you know my name?" Samuel stood, puzzled and perplexed. The wise old sage knew his name. What else did he know? Did he know why Samuel had come to see him?

"The question is not how I know your name, but why I know your name? It is no coincidence that we are meeting on the top of this mountain. You don't belong in Gloomsville."

"How do you know where I live? How much do you know about me? I know you're a wise old sage, but how could you possibly know that much about me?"

"Samuel, I know a great deal about you. Not by some mystical power or supernatural insight, but because of our relationship."

"I'm sorry, but I have never met you before. How could we have known each other before today?" Samuel was puzzled.

"Samuel, many years ago your father came to me asking how he could find happiness. He had never known happiness because he grew up in Gloomsville. He was so poisoned by pessimism and devoid of desire, ambition, courage, faith, and imagination. He had never known happiness but desperately wanted to experience it. I knew he was eager to find happiness, but by the same token, I knew he was not completely ready for it. If you've never had any happiness in your life and you try to force it, fake it, or quickly find it, you'll look for it in the wrong places and when you do find it, it won't last. Your father stayed here with me for almost a year. Everyday we worked together, talked together, and in the process I attempted to reprogram his thinking. You see, people who are bitter and angry hold on to their emotions because they don't know how to live without them.

They feel entitled to react to others' actions and words. All people feel anger and bitterness at some time, but only those who hold onto anger and bitterness become angry and bitter people."

"You knew my father old sage?"

"Please, Samuel, don't call me 'old sage'. My friends call me Sam. I've known your family for a very long time. You may not know your grandfather personally or any of your relatives, but you live in his village."

"Gompert Gloomberg, the man who founded Gloomsville is my grandfather?" Samuel was astonished and speechless. His father had never mentioned anything about any of his relatives at all.

"Yes, Samuel. He is. Your father grew up in the most miserable home in Gloomsville. He was also so lost when he came to live with me. He had never heard a positive word of encouragement in his life from anyone least of all his parents. He had no dreams and barely had an imagination for that matter. He was a completely lost soul. He had no ambitions, no skills, or talents because he had been treated like an unintelligent, unskilled, nobody. I spent the entire year trying to undo what his family had done to him. The problem is, you cannot completely undo in one year what has continuously been done over a lifetime."

"Your father thought he was ready to leave and find happiness. I knew he was not and continued to encourage him to stay another year with me but he would not. He had acquired ambition, but had not learned how to achieve true happiness. For a while it appeared that he was happy, but he had never had to find happiness and remain happy through difficult times and situations. That is why when things became difficult and trials came his way he returned to his former way of thinking."

"In life, Samuel, we each are challenged on a daily basis but it is how we face those challenges that determine our personal strength. Happiness does not come from careers, lifestyles, wealth, possessions, or even personal relationships. They can help contribute to our happiness, but happiness is innate. It is internal. It must come from within. You, my boy, have remained happy even in the worst conditions. You focus on positivity rather than negativity. Now tell me, why have you come to me Samuel?"

Samuel thought about that question for a while before responding. Just as Samuel was about to open his mouth to speak, the wise old sage burst into laughter.

"Why are you laughing, Sam?" Samuel had almost forgotten what happy laughter sounded like, but as he heard the wise old sage laugh, memories came flooding into his mind. A small smile lit up Samuel's face.

"My dear boy," began the wise old sage, "Is that a smile I see upon your face? You may not realize it, but you are smiling. How does it feel to smile? How does it make you feel?"

"Honestly Sam, right now I feel better than I have in years. I haven't smiled in years. Smiling makes me feel so good. Why is that? What does smiling do for me?" Samuel began to beam as his smile grew wider.

"Smiling is an important part of happiness. It makes you feel happy. As you smile you are subconsciously telling your brain to be happy and you're spreading happiness to others as well. When other people see you smile they automatically want to smile. It is a natural reaction." Samuel could see why Sam was called the 'wise old sage'.

"Sam, how have you learned so much about happiness?" As Samuel asked the question he watched the wise old sage very closely.

"Samuel, I have seen good times and bad times. I

have experienced the best and worst of both worlds. There was a time when my family was very happy. Unfortunately, there was a time when my family was very unhappy. My brother let his emotions get the better of him. He resigned to resent everyone and everything around him. He became very angry, bitter, and unhappy. Samuel, Gompert Gloomberg is my brother. I am your great uncle. When we were younger we had wonderful times together. Sadly, there was a tragedy in our family and my brother lost control. The worst part of a human being is the part that gives in, quits, rejects positivity, and chooses to find the worst in the rest of us. Gompert lost respect for humanity, but more than that, he lost respect for himself. He wanted to surround himself with others who felt as miserable and dejected toward life as he did. Sadly, I'm afraid he succeeded."

Everything made sense now. Samuel began to see the world differently. He had unknowingly been the victim of his grandfather's anger, but he could choose happiness.

"Samuel," the wise old sage began, "follow me to the peak of the mountain. I want to show you something." With that the wise old sage began walking up the mountain. Samuel followed behind his uncle until they reached the top.

"Look out at the beautiful valley below, my boy. There is so much beauty in the world. On the other side of the valley is the village your grandfather created. Now, let's look at the valley below. Look below us, what do you see?"

Once again Samuel examined the beautiful valley filled with trees, flowers, rivers, and lakes. It was absolutely breath-taking.

"Uncle, I see a beautiful valley filled with potential, possibilities, and happiness."

"Samuel, how would you describe the valley?"

"It's a beautiful and pleasant valley."

"Samuel, I named this valley 'Pleasantville' long before you were born. As children your grandfather and I played in amongst those aspen trees. We swam in those rivers and lakes. This valley is filled with so many fond and happy memories for me. It is peaceful and serene. It speaks of all that is good in the world."

"Samuel, I am giving this valley to you. I want you to build a city of possibility, of hope, peace, potential, productivity, and happiness. I want you to open your doors to the world and inspire others by your example. Welcome all who believe with open arms, acceptance, forgiveness, charity, and love. This valley will soon be one of the greatest cities on earth. It will be a place of refuge, hope, and happiness. The inhabitants will gladly work together, play together, laugh, sing, dance, create, uplift, inspire, and motivate each other to become better and to do their best. Samuel, this is your future. The world is filled with so many good people who need something to smile about, something to pray for, something to live for. Build this city in honor of the dreams dreamers dream. Give people something to look forward to and something that will make a difference in their lives and in the lives of their posterity."

Samuel surveyed the valley and dreamed about its potential. He and Sam, the wise old sage, began building Pleasantville, a city where pleasant people would live, dream, succeed, and smile.

The Brightest Star

A hush fell over the crowd of anxious onlookers. This was truly a marvelous day for the world to behold – for up in the sky was born a star to light the world.

This star's brilliance was praised as the brightest and most noble light any man had ever seen. This is the story of Sunny Star – the star of the Son.

Sunny was named after his grandfather, The Great Sun – the oldest, wisest, and brightest star little Sunny had ever heard of or seen.

Everyone loved being near Grandpa Sun because he was warm and friendly. It was said if you could get close to Grandpa, he might shed his light on you, and your own brilliance would increase. Little Sunny wanted to increase his brilliance. He wanted to shine and let others see and feel his light just like Grandpa Sun.

One day Sunny's little star friends were boasting about how bright they were. They made fun of little Sunny saying he didn't know how to shine. Laughing, they said, "Even a firefly gives off more light than Sunny."

Sunny felt hurt and embarrassed. He tried to show how wrong they were by giving off all the light he could.

"Look, Sunny is blushing," shouted one of the little stars.

"I am not," protested Sunny. "I'm letting my light shine." But as hard as he tried, he didn't really give off any light.

"That little Sunny thinks he can be a real star," whispered one of the older stars.

Sunny overheard what he said and raced away. He wanted to hide.

"No one likes me," whispered Sunny to the sky. "I am dim and I will never be bright like the other stars."

91

"Don't ever let me hear you say that again, little star," exclaimed a comet flying by.

"Who are you?", asked little Sunny.

"I am Cosmo the Great, but you can call me Coz. What's your name?"

"I'm Sunny Star."

"Sunny, have you ever seen people wish upon a star?"

"Yes, Coz, I have."

"Well, I am that star. I shoot through the sky and whenever people see me they make a wish."

"Coz, can I make my wish come true?"

"And what wish is that, Sunny?" Coz gently asked.

"I want to be the brightest star in the sky and shine for the whole world to see," Sunny blurted out.

Smiling, Coz said, "You know Sunny, I can see you need some help, but I personally have never been one for shining. My strength is speed. I do, however, have a star friend who is extremely bright and I know he can help you shine. He is "The Great Sun.""

"You know Grandpa Sun?" Sunny asked in disbelief.

"Of course I know him. I speed by him every day. We talk about the weather and I always let him know what's happening in other universes. We're pretty good friends. Climb aboard and I'll take you to see him."

Sunny and Coz sped across the sky. "Coz, look, there he is," shouted Sunny.

Grandpa Sun shimmered like gold, shooting beams of light in every direction. He had a happy smile and a hearty laugh.

"Grandpa Sun, my name is Sunny Star and I'm afraid I'm not a very good star." Sunny hung his head in shame.

"What makes you say that?" Grandpa Sun asked

Sunny with a twinkle in his eye.

"I don't really know how to shine like a star should. Everyone makes fun of me."

"My dear Sunny, you're just a little star. You mustn't compare yourself with the other stars. You can be as bright as you want."

"I want to be the brightest star in the sky and shine for the whole world to see," Sunny said.

"Sunny, you must understand that being bright and shiny is a gift you and I have received, but we must share our light with others for their enjoyment."

"But Grandpa you're the brightest and warmest star that has ever lived."

"My little star, how young you are. There is one who gives more light than I or any other star in the universe."

"Who is he, Grandpa?"

"He is our Heavenly Father, Sunny. He created you and me and everything in this universe."

"Grandpa, do you think He can teach me how to shine?"

"Yes, Sunny. In one moment He can teach you more about being a star than I could in a million years. Climb aboard Coz's back and he will take you to your Heavenly Father."

With that Sunny and Coz sped across the sky and came to a place unlike any Sunny had ever seen before.

"This is where our Heavenly Father lives," said Coz with pride.

Sunny looked around and saw beautiful streets of gold and castles in the clouds. Angels played harps of gold and sang heavenly songs.

All of a sudden Sunny saw who he knew must be Heavenly Father.

He was dressed in white – the most dazzling white Sunny had ever seen. His hair and beard were also a sparkling white.

"Cosmo, I see you've brought a little friend to see me. What a marvelous little star you are, Sunny."

Sunny was surprised that Heavenly Father knew his name, but Grandpa Sun did say Heavenly Father knew everything.

"Are you really the one who created everything?"

"Yes, Sunny, I did."

"Grandpa Sun told me you are brighter and warmer than anything in the universe."

"Your Grandpa and I are old friends."

"Heavenly Father, can you teach me how to shine?" Sunny asked. "I want to learn how to light up the sky. Grandpa said if I really want to shine I need to let my light help others."

Something had changed within Sunny. He was so dim before, but now he began to shine. He was bright.

"My little star," Heavenly Father said, "You have just learned the greatest lesson a star can learn. You only increase your light when you give it away. You can not be bright until you help others see the light."

Heavenly Father could see potential in this star and knew his heart was true. He could see the greatness in Sunny.

"Sunny, how would you like to be The Brightest Star? You said you want to shine and guide others until they receive the light. I need a star that can do that for me. This is the most important job any star could ever have. Will you be that star for me?"

Sunny thought for a moment and nodded. "Yes, Heavenly Father. I will."

"Sunny, I need you to light the sky for my Son. He

is going to be born in a manger and needs a bright star to announce his birth. Your light will guide others to Him. My Son is the light of the world, and I want you to be His star.

"Cosmo, take Sunny Star to his spot in the sky. My Son will be born tonight."

With that, Sunny jumped on Coz's back and they sped across the sky. He found his spot in the night sky and then beamed with all the energy he had, lighting up the entire world.

Sunny looked down and saw a small group of people gathered around an old stable. There were cows, and donkeys, and shepherds with their sheep. A young woman knelt in front of a manger and held a newborn baby boy in her arms.

This baby was the son of God, sent to be the light of the world, and Sunny felt so proud to have been the chosen star to let the world know of His birth.

An Ant Named Steed

Steed lived with the other ants in the ant hill by the forest, but Steed did not want to remain a worker in an ant hill. He had big dreams and imagined a beautiful ant hill of his own deep inside the forest near the flowers and trees. Every ant laughed at Steed and thought he was a dreamer. They often told him he should work as hard as he could in this ant hill and live his life as every other ant did. Steed couldn't believe every ant was happy being an ant. Of course he would work hard and do his best at what he did, he was, after all, an ant. Steed finally mustered up the courage to tell the other ants he was leaving for good. They all laughed. So Steed left. Years went by and Steed created the largest ant hill ever, deep inside the forest.

I'd Be Delighted

Dedicated to my father Jerry F. Simon
(Inspired by a true story)

Jerry liked to play baseball with the neighborhood boys, but Mom said there was work to be done on the farm.

Jerry wanted to play, but decided to do what Mom told him.

"Mom always said, 'Work is good for you.' And Dad always said, 'Nothing ever happens without work.'"

So Jerry went to work. The family was going to pick corn. The field was large and the rows never seemed to end. Everyone in the family was given their own row. Everyone that is – except Jerry.

"Jerry, I have something special in mind for you. I want you to fill this pail full of rocks," said Dad.

"Do I have to Dad? It's not as fun as picking corn."

"Jerry, sometimes work isn't always fun to do, but you can always have fun doing it."

"What do you mean?" Jerry asked.

"Anytime anyone asks me to do something, I say, 'I'd be delighted.' It makes me feel good because then I don't see it as work," Dad said. "I'm just helping people. Jerry, just say – 'I'd be delighted' and you'll feel better. Jerry, I promise you will."

Jerry stood in front of a pile of rocks, and looked down at his pail.

Then Jerry whispered, "I'd be delighted," and picked up a rock.

He felt different when he said the words. "It worked," thought Jerry to himself. And then he picked up another rock.

"Dad, I felt something when I picked up the rock. I've never felt it before. What was it?" Jerry shouted at his Dad who was picking corn.

"You probably felt good even though you're doing something that isn't very fun, Jerry. Whenever you say 'I'd be delighted' everything seems easier and the day goes by quicker than before. You're having fun working and you never thought you could, did you, Jerry?"

Jerry didn't answer his dad. Jerry was busy looking at his pail and the pile of rocks. He smiled and picked up another rock and put it in his pail. Once again he whispered 'I'd be delighted' and he felt so good.

"Whenever anyone asks me to help around the house I'm going to say this special phrase 'I'd be delighted' and help them."

From then on Jerry was always helpful and always felt good doing work around the house because he always remembered to say 'I'd be delighted'. And he always was delighted.

The Members of the Rosebush Family

The members (or parts) of the Rose Bush family had an interesting discussion one day. The roses, in their grandeur, said they were the most important feature of the rose bush. The petals, the stems, and the thorns protested and said they each had important roles. Without their help the roses couldn't survive. One rose, in particular, vehemently denounced the worth of each petal, stem, and thorn.

"I don't need any of you to help me survive and don't want you near me. You're not at all beautiful. I only want to be surrounded by beauty." The angry rose was serious and meant it.

One of the stems said, "Without me you'd surely shrivel up and die. You can't live without me and won't survive for very long without me. If you feel you no longer need me, I will stop giving you the nourishment you need and will, instead, help a new rose bloom."

"Fine!," retorted the self-righteous rose. "I'll be better off without you anyway," she added.

And so with that, the stem stopped sending nourishment to the haughty rose and, of course, she withered and died.

Each of us are members of our own "rosebush" family. We all have very important roles to play. We cannot survive without each other, and yet, often times we can feel and act like the haughty rose. That can be our downfall and our own personal destruction. We do it to ourselves, but at the same time, we hurt those around us. We need to change and all work together and realize that we all need and rely on each other.

The Beetle and The Praying Mantis

A beetle and praying mantis were working in the field together. The beetle was feeling overworked and under-appreciated. Sensing the beetles' frustration, the praying mantis politely asked, "why are you so sad, friend?"

The beetle quickly replied, "I don't like all this work. I don't like being out here in the heat of the day slaving away and then receiving a small compensation for the work I've done. I'm going to quit."

"You mustn't," replied the praying mantis. "If you do, you may not work again."

"I was born working and I will die working. I don't mind the work or the conditions, but I don't like being undervalued, under-appreciated, and underemployed. I'm willing to do more work but I want to be compensated accordingly," complained the beetle.

"Have you told the chief beetle you'd like a heavier workload and that you'd like to be compensated accordingly for the added work you'll be doing?"

"No I haven't," answered the beetle calmly.

"If you think you can handle more and do a good job with the extra work load, you will be compensated and rewarded for your work. The head beetle will see your commitment and dedication to the work you do. If I were you, I'd ask what more needs to be done and then do it, in the beginning, without an increase in compensation. Take initiative. When they see what a good job you are doing with an increased work load and the enthusiasm and energy you show everyday, I'm sure they will value you more, appreciate you more, and you'll be compensated accordingly," counseled the praying mantis.

And from that day on the beetle did exactly that.

The Knight of Nobility

There once was a brave old knight named Tristan who lived deep in the heart of the forest. He was affectionately known as "Sir Tristan the Great." Many young knights would often visit the wise old knight and ask him for advice.

Gerard was a noble young knight who came to a series of crossroads in his young life and needed direction. He set out on a long and treacherous journey deep into the heart of the forest to visit the brave old knight.

"Tell me, young noble knight, why have you come to visit me deep in the heart of my forest?" Sir Tristan examined the eager youth and waited for his reply.

"My wise brave knight," Gerard began, "I need more courage, more bravery, and more strength. I want to be the best knight in all the land."

Wise old Tristan carefully thought about his response to the hopeful young knight.

"My young knight, there's more to knighthood than courage and bravery and strength. Much more. What are the desires of your heart? What is your purpose and reason for life? What is your mission and what are your immediate and long term goals?"

Gerard was taken aback. He hadn't planned on hearing such words from Sir Tristan. Gerard had no response to any of the questions asked of him. He was speechless.

"My wise knight, isn't bravery and strength a noble and virtuous aspiration for any knight?"

"My young friend, the truly important aspects in life often cannot be seen: faith, love, intelligence, humility, charity, purity, virtue, patience, wisdom, and character. Are these not the most noble and virtuous quests in life?

"Should we not as noble knights live a higher law and seek to help others do the same? Knight Gerard, I will send you on a quest to acquire some of these most noble gifts of life. The ones you must acquire first to help you on your journey are humility, patience, faith, love, and intelligence and wisdom. The other virtues, charity, purity, and character cannot be given to you or perfectly taught to you - they must be lived. You must earn them and re-earn them over a lifetime. They must be kept, guarded, and protected throughout your life."

"But, Sir Tristan the Great," Knight Gerard began, "obviously, as you can see, I do not need too much more intelligence or wisdom."

Sir Tristan the Great burst into unbridled laughter.

"My foolish knight, you have quickly shown me how little you do know and how much you need to learn. You are very young. Your thoughtless remark shows me how lacking in intelligence or wisdom you truly are and these two areas are only surpassed by your complete lack of humility. I apologize for being so bold and outspoken, and for laughing the way I did, but you must listen to me and respect my counsel if you truly want to change and become a noble knight. You have much to learn and we have very little time. You will be leaving in the morning to visit my friend, Garland, the Invisible Knight."

"But, if he is truly invisible, how will I see him?"

"Gerard, you will not see him until he has seen you and determined who you are and what strengths and weaknesses you have. A few moments in your presence will tell him everything he needs to know about you."

With that, Sir Tristan the Great showed knight Gerard where he would stay and sleep for the evening.

Knight Gerard didn't sleep at all. His mind wouldn't let him, and also the straw bed was scratchy and uncomfortable.

He might have slept better if he had laid on the rocky floor of the stable where the great old war horses were kept.

At the break of dawn, Sir Tristan excitedly arose, quickly dressed, and walked purposefully to the point where the sun crept over the mountain landscape. He then took out an ornate gold horn and blew a beautiful melody to greet the day and arouse the sleepy servants and handmaidens who worked on his land. Knight Gerard watched the remarkable, almost ceremony-like event with wonder and awe. Later that morning breakfast was eaten and Sir Tristan the Great embraced Gerard and wished him well on his journey and adventure. Gerard thought it odd that he would use the word adventure, but he had no idea what lay in store for him as he embarked on the greatest quest of his life. This quest would change the way he viewed the world and more important, the way he viewed himself, who he had been, who he was, and who he could become.

Knight Gerard marched on with purpose for what seemed like days. He didn't know where he was going and had been told to head East until the Eastern sky embraced him. He didn't even know what that meant. He did not know what to think of his encounter with Sir Tristan the Great, but did know that he was a mighty man and a great and noble knight. He believed Sir Tristan's words and hoped to meet Garland, the Invisible Knight.

Knight Gerard rode on for days and finally stopped at the edge of a beautiful lake nestled outside a thick grove of trees. He camped for a night and a day and decided to enter the trees. Upon entering the forest off the west bank of the blue waters, Knight Gerard heard a faint cough coming from a bush ten or so feet in front of him. He cautiously approached the overgrown weed and then heard footsteps behind him. Carefully turning around, he peered over his right shoulder and saw nothing. A tree branch broke to his left and Knight Gerard whirled around in a circle, all the while fumbling for his sword which was awkwardly stuck in its sheath.

"You must be my new protégé," laughed a hearty voice directly above Gerard.

Knight Gerard saw nothing.

"My friend did tell you I was invisible, did he not?"

The frightened knight nodded his head in all directions while darting back and forth. Once again, that boisterous laughter erupted and grew louder.

"I can't take any more of this comical turning about this way and that like a mad man."

The familiar laughter grew louder as Garland the Invisible Knight appeared before Knight Gerard's eyes.

"Take a good look, my young friend. You may not see me for a while and in a short period of time you may never see me again."

"Didn't Sir Tristan the Great tell you a knight would be visiting you? I am he," bellowed Knight Gerard. He often spoke with great force every syllable he uttered as if it made more of an impact on those about him.

"Why do you roar when you speak? Simply speak to me as one man speaketh to another. There is no need to yell when I am only a few feet away. You are not acting on some stage. Do not pretend to put on a show for others. Never be something you are not or pretend to be someone else, or what you imagine someone else to be. Simply be yourself. That is the first counsel I extend."

"Next," Garland continued, I would have you look at yourself and examine yourself as you are today. Don't think about past victories or future fears. We will address them in a minute. For now, only focus on you as you are right this very moment. What you see and what I see are two very different people. You might look at me and quickly see my weaknesses and shortcomings, yet you are very slow to look at yourself and see your own weaknesses, imperfections, and defects. If you do see them, or think they exist, you do not acknowledge them at all and have not taken any time to do anything about them or make any corrections or attempts to change. Am I not correct in my initial assumption of you?"

Knight Gerard was confounded. He was utterly speechless again and didn't know what to think, let alone what to say.

"I take your silence to be shock and disbelief that constrains and forbids you to tell me how you *really* feel and what you *really* think. And you are doing that because you fear what I may say next. The truth, my friend, is very liberating and is profoundly powerful. If we are truthful with ourselves and with everyone else, we will never fear what tomorrow will bring because we will have lived exemplary lives that were always lived in the light. Those who do any deed of darkness, in action or thought, must continually retrace their steps and recreate their past because most of their successes and failures are half truths and exaggerated claims of a life well lived. Most people think too highly of themselves and not highly enough of others. A few, sadly, are plagued with the reverse scenario and don't think highly enough of themselves to live life as it should be lived and prefer to hide away in the shadows of sadness. You, of course, do not have that problem. But a little humility wouldn't hurt you. The time is now yours to speak freely, openly, and without restraint. What do you want to learn, my young friend? The teacher presents himself when the student appears and only when the student is ready to learn. You have traveled a great distance and have sacrificed much for this experience. I know the great effort involved in coming here. The greatest rewards demand the most sacrifices. Life is an experience where we learn and grow. You are determined and I willingly share my counsel and advice with everyone who is determined and dedicated to improve. I want pupils who aren't afraid to work and want to be honest with themselves and with others. Are you willing to do what is asked of you in order to change and become the Knight you long to be?"

Knight Gerard slowly nodded.

"Then speak on, my friend! What seekest thou in my forest?" Garland, the Invisible Knight, stood before Knight Gerard in plain sight and looked at him with encouraging eyes that commanded a response.

"Sir Tristan the Great said I must first acquire humility, then patience, faith, love, and intelligence, and wisdom. He then said that the other virtues: charity, purity, and character cannot be given to me or perfectly taught to me. He said I must live them and must earn them and re-earn them over a lifetime, that I must keep, guard, and protect them throughout my life. If I must learn all of these traits to become a great knight, then I will do whatever is asked of me. I am not afraid to work. Although it is difficult to hear my faults spoken openly and honestly, I am willing to do what it takes to make my weaknesses become strengths. I know I am not perfect even though I pretend to be so at times. I will try not to do that anymore." Knight Gerard genuinely seemed a more gentle man - someone more approachable and reachable.

"My friend, I see a calming change in you - one I did not see when first we met. My words, though somewhat hurtful to you, did cause some reflection on your part, and that is good. You have been humbled temporarily and I hope it continues to last. When we think we have become something or are in the process of becoming something or someone in our own eyes or even - and especially - in the eyes of our peers, that is when life catches up to us and gently reminds us that we are human. Sometimes we receive a not-so-friendly reminder. We have weaknesses, temptations, faults, pains, and problems. Everyone has these difficulties and that is okay. We shouldn't pretend we don't. It doesn't do anyone any good to pretend they are something or someone they are not. For this reason, humility is the first trait we present to our students who seek a change of heart and a change of lifestyle."

"What do you mean by saying a change of lifestyle?" Knight Gerard looked on in a quizzical and overwhelmed manner.

"My dear friend, and I hope we become true friends, for dear and true friends are difficult to come by these days - if you truly have a change of heart you will ultimately have a change of lifestyle. Your life will never be the same again and it shouldn't be. In fact, there is no way it can be. You will, in a very real sense of the expression, become a new person. Your former self will become but a memory as you change for the better and improve. You see, that is why we encourage headstrong and immature young men to become knights. It is a right of passage and an opportunity for the youth to put off childish thoughts and attitudes toward life. They are changed and if they focus on learning and embracing patience, developing faith, learning to love and be loved, and honestly seek true intelligence, then they will find wisdom. You will soon learn that wisdom is acquiring real knowledge from real life situations. It is the practical application of the knowledge you learn from teachers, books, philosophies, creeds, friends and foes. The practical application of that knowledge shows itself in the form of wisdom. But wisdom is not enough. Knowing and doing is good, but it is not good enough. We must become men of honor, valor, and worth, and our character involves what we do day in and day out when surrounded by the masses or even when we are alone and think no one is watching us. Even if no one really is watching us - as noble knights, we remain the same and are true to principles we have learned. We must have values and some higher standard by which we live our lives. It is about being and becoming men of character. The same is true of women. All women can and should become ladies and princesses. They all are of royal birth, just as the men are, but some, like the men, forget. You must never forget who you are."

"Life is about discovering who we can and should be and become. This encompasses the higher virtues: charity, purity, and character. Our character is the summation and compilation of our beliefs, actions, knowledge and wisdom. Combined together, these attributes become our principles of prosperity and prepare us to face the challenges of each day."

"May I call you Gerard? Please, I would prefer it if you called me Garland. Garland the Invisible Knight is such a lengthy title for friends."

Garland looked at Gerard and asked him what his thoughts were. Overwhelmed and completely caught off guard, Gerard simply said: "I...I really need to think about all of this. It's so much to take in in such a short amount of time."

"We have so much more to cover and I don't want to move on if you are not ready." Garland smiled and nodded encouragingly at Gerard.

To Gerard's credit, he was actually listening - even intently. It was something he was not accustomed to doing. More often than not, he simply exclaimed to the world what he thought and hoped he would accomplish, do, or be. He often spoke without first thinking things through.

107

This was all new to Gerard, but it was something he knew he would need to master.

"Garland, how does one discover who he can and should be and become?" asked Gerard. "I have lived so long pursuing the quests others have given me, that I have never actually thought about what I would like from life." Gerard was beaming as if this new concept was revolutionary.

"Life is all about discovery, my friend." Garland spoke with such strength and conviction. He never hesitated, paused, or even questioned anything he said. It was as if every word he spoke had been rehearsed and polished to perfection. "Do you know what you want out of life? Do you know who you are?" The once invisible knight's comment was compelling and somewhat confusing.

Knight Gerard asked, "How can anyone know what they want out of life? Isn't life about learning and continuing to grow? Is there ever an end to the quests we must take?" Gerard looked on for comfort and counsel.

"Now you are asking the correct questions. You see, each day is a gift of personal discovery. We continue to change and grow as new challenges present themselves to us. We face opportunities and obstacles every minute of every day. We then are given a glimpse into ourselves - our level of understanding, our ability to adapt and improve, or our inability to change for the better. We are continually changing. Change allows us to see ourselves as we are, based on the choices we have made, for better or for worse. Everything we do brings with it a chain reaction that propels us forward or holds us back."

The light from the stars began shimmering through the dark green leaves of the surrounding trees. The two knights had been asking and answering each others questions all afternoon and late into the evening. The sun had long ago set and now the crescent moon shone overhead as twinkling stars lit up the sky.

"I think it is time for us to retire, my new and much younger friend," Garland announced mid-yawn while brushing his eyes with the backs of his callused hands.

"I could go on for hours. There are so many questions I have and answers I long to receive." Gerard looked on hoping to convince Garland to stay a little longer.

"It is good you now have a desire to learn and grow. That is a step in the right direction. But Heaven knows I need what little beauty sleep I deserve - though little it may be. Think about the questions and ponder the answers you hope to receive. Part of the adventure is in asking and the other part is in receiving answers to questions you never asked." Garland smiled a sly smile and quickly vanished into thin air.

"But, what does that mean? How can I receive answers when I don't ask any questions? Garland, are you there? Are you going to leave me out here in this dark forest by myself?"

"Listen to the whispering wind, my friend. It will answer the questions you ask. But you must ask the right questions, or the wind will wail and moan and never leave you alone." And with those final parting words, Garland was gone.

"What wind? There isn't any wind. Why have I been left alone in the dark in the middle of a forest? Did I mention I was alone? I have no one to talk to but myself out here. What is with these cryptic messages? Sir Tristan told me to head East until the Eastern sky embraced me. Now you tell me to listen to the whispering wind. What is this? Are you there? Why am I talking to myself if no one is listening?"

The forest was so quiet and yet so alive at the same time. Gerard was all alone with his thoughts. It felt as if he stood completely alone in the world. He knew that was not true, but it felt to him as though he was the only one alive for hundreds of miles in all directions.

"Maybe I should talk to myself," Gerard mumbled out loud to himself. "I mean, what is wrong with talking to myself anyway? If I can't feel comfortable talking with myself and working through problems on my own, how can I expect to help others or even receive help from others? Maybe I need to get to know myself better and discover what I am doing with my life. I haven't always been the best at communicating my feelings and thoughts the way I would like. I know most people struggle with that, so I am by no means alone in how I act. But if I am going to be completely honest with myself, I am rarely honest with myself. I do put up my defenses and even put on a show for everyone around me. Why do I do that? Am I afraid to be me? Am I afraid to let people see who I really am? Do I even know who I really am or am I still searching for me?"

With that, a gust of wind picked up and hurled leaves and branches all around. Dirt flew through the air and debris was thrown in all directions. Gerard quickly ran to find his stallion and search for protection from the storm. It hadn't started raining, but the winds were quite fierce. After riding for a few hours in the darkest part of the forest, Gerard found a cave in a secluded spot on the far end of the forest. Quickly taking safety within the cave and securing his horse in one end of the cave, Knight Gerard went to the mouth of the castle-like cave and watched the sky begin to drench the surrounding area with enormous raindrops, much larger than any raindrops Gerard had seen before. The wind began to howl and even scream, as if weeping and mourning the loss of someone or something.

"Why does the wind wail and moan? It sounds mournful? Is the earth responding to some great misfortune or loss? What is happening within this forest?" Confusion settled in quite rapidly as Gerard tried to think. Nothing was clear and everything seemed to make no sense. The forest seemed so much darker than he remembered.

Had the wind heard Garland the Invisible? Was it responding to his will? Did Sir Tristan and Garland the Invisible have some mystical and magical power over the elements that Knight Gerard knew nothing about? It was all so difficult to comprehend. Everything seemed to be spinning and Gerard felt tired and queasy. "Maybe the world will make more sense if I can rest for a few moments and clear my mind of this darkness." After speaking these words Gerard abruptly fell asleep. It was a very deep and calming sleep at first.

Knight Gerard awoke in a panic. It was morning and the sun was rising. He was sweating profusely and the perspiration felt like fire. He sat up, turned and saw his horse to his left, who understandably was a little startled to see the sight of Gerard, but also eager to be fed nonetheless.

"I just had the most horrific nightmare imaginable! I dreamed I saw myself and every past mistake I have ever made. They were piled up all around me, miles and miles of mistakes." Gerard looked around and realized he was talking to himself again, or at least to his horse. The funny thing was, it seemed his horse nodded in agreement as if he understood. Was Gerard imagining he saw this?

Knight Gerard continued talking to himself and his trusty stallion. "In this nightmare I saw how my actions and words had affected others. I guess I never really thought about other people very much because I was always thinking about me and my wants and needs. But in this dream not only did I see every single mistake I have made throughout my life, I also saw what happened to those around me who were affected by my behavior. I don't think I ever really thought about it like that before, but every negative act of mine had many negative repercussions. Each one was more severe and hurtful than the one before."

"That is also true of your thoughts as well," said a familiar and much welcomed voice. Garland had reappeared and was calmly grooming the horse and brushing the stallion's mane.

"Garland, you have returned. I am so glad to see you because last night was one of the most horrible and painful nights of my life. You would not believe the terrible dream I had. Thankfully, it was only a dream."

"Oh, it was no dream, of that I am sure. The winds were wailing and moaning, were they not? The winds merely carried to you the cries of others because of your actions, words, and thoughts." As Garland finished his piercing statement he looked at Knight Gerard and nodded while allowing the horse to eat a shiny red apple he had brought.

"Do you mean to tell me the nightmare I experienced is real - that *I* am the cause of so much pain and suffering for so many?" Knight Gerard whispered this in unbelief.

"Each of us causes far too much pain and suffering both knowingly and unknowingly. This happens because of what we do, what we say and think, and also because of what we believe and feel about ourselves and others. It's terrible what our thoughts can do to us and so many others. It can also happen when we do not do or say or think or believe something we should. Some refer to these as sins of commission *and* omission. Both are detrimental and quite deadly. The things we do not do but should are just as damaging as the things we do and should not do."

"Why do you always speak in riddles, Garland? Are we accountable for the things we do not think, say and do but should, in addition to the things we actually do? Surely not, for people all over the world do and say things and even think things that are offensive and hurtful all the time. I am not alone in my thinking and actions. Many agree with me and would argue with you on this subject. And what does it matter anyway? I personally think too many people are too easily offended. Some of us do and say things just for fun and in jest. All knights at times speak ill of others or gossip about one another's weaknesses and limitations. It's human nature. We all do it and I don't see anything wrong with that. I'm sure you have heard of Marlo the Magnificent Knight. Even he, the great knight, mocks and makes fun of others and often speaks negatively of others behind their back - but we are all human and that is in our nature. If he who is the greatest and strongest knight in all the land can speak ill of others on occasion and at times do what is not honest or fair to others, than why should it be any different for the rest of us? All other knights long to be like he is for there is none greater. Don't you agree, Garland? I am sure you know of him and his greatness."

"I do know of him but he is not great in the least and you should not seek to follow in his footsteps, Gerard."

"But Marlo the Magnificent Knight is the most respected and revered knight in all the land. His castles are the finest and most spacious buildings round about and are all filled with the greatest luxuries wealth can buy. He is also the strongest knight of any kingdom. Everyone strives to do as he does. What is wrong with that? He is a hero to many!"

"My dear young knight," Garland began, "Do you always compare yourself with others? You have stated that this knight is the most respected and revered knight in all the land and that he is very wealthy and essentially has everything money can buy. You speak of him as a hero, is that correct?"

"Yes, Garland, everyone praises his name and longs to live the kind of lifestyle he lives. He is aptly named 'The Magnificent', because there is no one quite like him. I have always wanted to follow in his footsteps." Knight Gerard now began thinking more thoroughly about how Marlo the Magnificent didn't always do what he should and often did get into a little trouble here and there because he cheated a little, lied every now and then, and he always did everything that was in his own best interest.

"Knight Gerard, why do people strive to be like this knight if he mocks them and speaks ill of them behind their back. You said yourself that everyone does that. Why is that? And if you are dishonest even a little, how can you justify deceiving others when you are only deceiving yourself? This is especially true even if no one else knows what you have done, said, or even thought. You are the one who must live with yourself and your decisions. How can you make it through a lifetime with others if you cannot make it through one day with yourself and your own thoughts? If you are honest with yourself then truth will be your path and happiness will be your destination. But if you are dishonest with yourself, how can you truly be honest with anyone else?"

Garland the Invisible Knight stopped speaking and allowed the silence to penetrate Knight Gerard as silence always does. The absence of speaking often produces very effective thinking. Garland watched as Knight Gerard collapsed on the rock beside his faithful steed.

"So my actions and my words can hurt people and unless I guard myself against myself, I can both knowingly and unknowingly hurt those around me - both neighbors and friends." Gerard looked down at his hands and felt guilt pour over him like the downpour of a depressing deluge.

"Gerard, we must watch our actions, our words, *and* our thoughts. Many times our thoughts are much more damaging than our words or our actions ever could be."

"Now I can't believe that," Knight Gerard bellowed at the top of his lungs.

"It's true. The thought plane is very real and does exist. Our negative thoughts hurt us and others as we think them. Just as our positive thoughts elevate our thinking and help us focus on faith, hope, and being our best in the present and the future, so likewise do our negative thoughts tear us and those around us down." Garland looked at Gerard and hoped he was understanding everything.

"But how can my thoughts hurt others?," pled Gerard.

"They can hurt ourselves and others because thoughts create positive and negative energy. This is nothing new. Just as we have sound waves, we also have thought waves. We are encircled about each day by thought waves - our own and those of others. Thoughts can bring us down or lift us up. It is entirely what we choose to think about and is often affected by the thoughts, both positive and negative, that others are thinking about us as well. As we think a thought, it instantly sends a message to our brain to focus intently on the mood that the thought produces. Each thought has a certain mood attached to it. That mood creates a chemical change within our bodies that either stimulates us and encourages us to accomplish more, and be more, or depletes us of energy altogether and brings down upon us a depression of our own making."

"You see, Gerard," The invisible knight continued, "We can instantly feel when something isn't quite right. You know when someone is angry or upset with you because of their actions and words. But their words and actions are the result of their thoughts. The thoughts others think about us are in a very real way sent to us through this thought plane and we can feel something about another person without them saying a word to us. The hair on your arms may rise or you may have a chill course down your spine when you feel something is not right. Those feelings are being transmitted to your thoughts from the thoughts of others. We all think and are connected to the thought plane."

"Garland, it's funny you should say all of this because right before you arrived I was talking to myself and actually thought my horse was listening to and understanding everything I was saying and even every thought I was thinking."

"It's because he was," said Garland with a sly smile and a small wrinkle in his nose, as he looked into the eyes of the great steed.

"What do you mean *he* was?" questioned Gerard with a look of complete disbelief. "I wasn't serious!"

"Every human and every creature that walks upon the face of this earth is connected to the thought plane. Animals know when you are afraid. They sense it because your thoughts are instantly communicated to them. But not only the animals - all living trees, flowers, and bodies of water, have souls, and each is connected to you as you are connected to them. What a glorious day it will be when you can kneel down beside a flower and hear its beautiful song or listen and understand what the birds are chirping about. If you can distance yourself from yourself and think more about other people and your surroundings, including nature, then you will connect with nature and other people around you on a much deeper level. Now, the day is slipping away from us and you have much to do. Our talks have been wonderful and I think you have learned enough for now. It is time, I believe, to send you on a great quest to slay your personal dragons."

"But Garland, we are just starting to talk and get somewhere. I feel as if I am beginning to understand and see things more clearly. Please don't leave me now. I have so much more I need to learn and understand. I need to spend more time learning from you. You said the teacher presents himself when the student is willing. I *am* willing. Please don't stop now. And besides, what dragons must I face anyway? I don't want to face any of them without your knowledge and strength. I need your help! Please don't go! Stay!"

"Knight Gerard, you can learn a great deal from me but you can learn even more from yourself. I know your strengths and weaknesses just as you do, and if you are completely honest with yourself, you can examine your thoughts, your words, and your actions and determine if they are helping you and those around you or if they are hurting others and doing more damage than good. You were initially told that you must acquire humility, patience, faith, love, intelligence, and wisdom followed by the other virtues of charity, purity, and character. Already, you have shown great humility to talk with yourself and learn about your weaknesses and strengths. This is a good start, but you must now conquer and slay the dragons of impatience, fear, hatred, and ignorance. These are the opposites of patience, faith, love, and intelligence. Until you face these four dragons, you will continue to wander in self doubt and pity. You will remain lost. After you slay these dragons you will receive the gift of wisdom. It is a gift that can only come to you as you live and make decisions that are directed by faith, love, and intelligence. Now go face your dragons!"

And with that Garland the Invisible once again disappeared. Knight Gerard felt completely alone. He didn't even voice his frustration as he thought Garland must already sense his thoughts through the thought plane. To make matters even worse, Gerard looked over at his horse and felt his horse was judging him. He could no longer look at another animal, tree, plant, or body of water in the same way again. His thoughts had completely changed. He knew they were all thinking, living entities.

After sitting alone and pondering on his exchange with Garland the Invisible, Knight Gerard mustered the courage to stand up and in a loud voice proclaimed:

"I am ready to face my dragons if that is what it will take. Where are the dragons of my soul?"

Almost immediately he heard or perhaps thought he heard Sir Tristan the Great's voice come into his mind. At first it was a whisper and then it grew louder and louder until it rang in Gerard's ears.

"He who is patient can withstand the tests of time."

"What on earth does that even mean?," exclaimed the almost dumbfounded knight.

"I said I am ready to face the dragons of my soul."

Once again, Knight Gerard roared his thunderous response and looked heavenward and all about.

"If you cannot control your thoughts and words, you will never be ready to face the dragons that hide within you," pronounced the familiar voice of Sir Tristan the Great. This time there was no mistaking his voice.

"Sir Tristan, It is I, Knight Gerard, and I am ready to go to battle. Let me fight so I might prove myself to thee and all others." Knight Gerard finished speaking and looked on waiting for a response from the great knight. Sir Tristan remained invisible, but his voice rang throughout the land.

"My young Knight," began Sir Tristan the Great as he appeared behind Gerard - "You must get to know yourself as you never have before. No one can accompany you. This is a battle you must face on your own. The knights who truly are the most prepared to go to battle are the ones who never need to fight. If you were as ready as you should be you would not need to prove yourself to anyone other than yourself. It does not matter what others around you think about you. If your thoughts are pure and noble, you will never need to question the thoughts and intents of others. If they are good you will see the fruits of their labors and will partake in the bounty of their blessings. If their thoughts are negative and dark, you will be protected by your positivity and you will be continually surrounded by light. Darkness will have no power over you because the illumination of happiness will encircle you and protect you - even from yourself when necessary."

"Sir Tristan," Knight Gerard began, "Why do all of the great knights speak in riddles and parables? Can you not speak plainly to me as others do so that I may easily understand you?"

"Knight Gerard, if I spoke plainly to you in your present understanding of the world as you know it, you would not pay as much attention to my words, nor would you believe them. You still think yourself superior to all others and would view my words as inferior. For this reason I speak plainly for those who are ready to hear the counsel they need. You cannot yet understand with clarity because your mind is still set on doing things as you always have. You believe my words are cloaked in cleverness, but you do not realize that we speak what is true and if you know and follow the truth, it will set you free. You want light, but continue to embrace darkness."

Once again, Knight Gerard had no comeback and did not know what to say. His thoughts were racing and he had difficulty keeping up with them.

"Please help me learn to be patient with myself and others. Please help me be better, Sir Tristan. I know I can improve and grow but I need your help," whispered Knight Gerard. There was an even deeper level of humility and sincerity in his words. He was calmer now and started acting more real than ever before in his life. There was a mighty change in the young knight.

"Knight Gerard," spoke Sir Tristan the Great with much conviction and purpose, "Arise and take my hand. Today you face the dragons of your past. You are prepared and will conquer the demons within you."

And with that, Knight Gerard took Sir Tristan's hand and instantly the two vanished. A second later Knight Gerard found himself alone within a great castle surrounded by four of the fiercest looking dragons he had ever seen. Once again he heard the voice of Garland the Invisible.

"Knight Gerard, now is the time to conquer and slay the dragons of impatience, fear, hatred, and ignorance. As I mentioned before, these are the opposites of patience, faith, love, and intelligence. They surround you and attack you every day. If you do not stand up to them, they will destroy you. These are your enemies - not man. They are the enemies of your soul. Conquer them and you shall walk in light, love, and happiness. If they destroy you then you will be filled with darkness, hatred, and sadness. Go. Fight them and prove yourself to yourself."

"But there are too many," complained Knight Gerard. "I am completely outnumbered and alone. Please help me fight them." Knight Gerard was filled with fear!

"Know we are with you and always will be, our young, brave knight. You have never been alone and never will be. But you must fight these demons on your own. We will give you our strength, but you must fight these dragons for they are *your* dragons. Only you have the power to destroy them."

This time it was Sir Tristan the Great who spoke and offered comforting counsel. At that very moment one of the larger, more scaly dragons, the dragon of impatience, breathed out a flame of fire that nearly scorched Gerard.

"But there are too many," complained Knight Gerard as he quickly leapt backwards to avoid being consumed by fire. In jumping back he fell over a large shiny shield. "I am completely outnumbered and alone. Please help me fight them." At that moment, Knight Gerard was filled with terror!

"Remember my words," exclaimed Garland. "Until you face these four dragons, you will continue to wander in self doubt and pity. You cannot doubt yourself. You cannot feel sorry for yourself. Everyone has dragons and many have some much worse than yours but everyone must stand and face them. Arise and be a Knight of Nobility!" Gerard felt Garland's strength and courage.

And with that, Gerard quickly arose and whispered to himself, "I believe in myself." In doing so and because he quickly arose and walked toward the dragon of impatience, the formidable beast quickly vanished.

"What just happened, Garland?," questioned Gerard.

"You took action, my friend and quickly rose to the challenge. You waited until you were ready and then when you were ready, you did not hesitate, so the dragon of impatience could not remain in your presence, for you showed you will not allow it." Garland appeared in the flesh before Gerard and patted him on the arm with a grandfatherly sense of adoration.

"That was all it took?," stammered Gerard in disbelief.

"Quickly fight the rest," shouted Sir Tristan, "You are not finished yet!"

Knight Gerard turned with greater confidence to face the other dragons.

"The dragon of impatience vanished because I was patient and then took action." Knight Gerard had become accustomed to speaking to himself and felt more at ease in conversing with himself by this point.

"Before acting on what I told myself I should do," Gerard continued, "I told myself that I believed in myself. Maybe that is the first step - to believe that I can accomplish anything I encounter. Regardless of the obstacles or challenges presented before me, If I believe I can do it, maybe that belief will empower me to act and bring to pass in the physical realm what my thoughts have already created in the thought plane. I do believe that thoughts are actual entities and become real and tangible as I focus intently and intensely on them."

And with those words and on that thought, Gerard walked courageously up to the dragon of fear and with great faith he boldly declared:

"I have faith in myself and my abilities to overpower whatever fears may come my way. I know I am not alone and will not fight my battles by myself for Sir Tristan the Great and Garland the Invisible shall forever walk beside me. Their knowledge is my knowledge. Their strength is my strength. Their faith is my faith and I know that if I have faith I will not fear."

With that pronouncement the dragon of fear roared and bellowed an ugly and horrific beastly sound while fire and smoke puffed out its nostrils and ears.

"Stand tall, young knight and do not be afraid." Sir Tristan knew he needed to encourage the young knight as everyone needs encouragement especially at the most frightening and difficult times in life.

Sir Tristan's words encouraged and empowered the knight to stand taller and look the dragon of fear in the eyes.

"I choose to embrace faith and forsake fear. You have no place in my life. Be gone and let me be!" Knight Gerard spoke with conviction and power. He was not the same knight who had entered the forest a short while back.

Knight Gerard looked at the dragon and the dragon instantly went up in a pillar and puff of smoke. He was gone.

"You are the most worthless knight I have ever met and will never amount to anything!" yelled the dragon of hatred. Hearing a dragon speak had startled Knight Gerard, because he didn't know dragons could speak. This one was filled with intense hatred.

"You can only destroy the dragon of hate with love," shouted Garland the Invisible who had once again disappeared from view.

"How do I love something I hate so much." Gerard felt so confused.

"Tell him you love him. Don't hate him or anyone for that matter. Learn to love everyone." This time Sir Tristan gave the advice.

"But I don't," shouted Gerard. And with that the dragon of hatred grew larger and became more fierce and foreboding.

"Hate breeds more hatred. Only love can stop the hate. Only love will protect you from the hatred of others and from the hatred within yourself. You must love those who hate you and you must learn to love yourself." Sir Tristan always spoke with love and was surrounded by so much light.

"I must learn to love myself," thought knight Gerard. "I must learn to love those who hate me and dispel their hatred with my love," exclaimed Knight Gerard out loud.

With these words the dragon began to shrink down to Gerard's size. Gerard continued and spoke gently and with more love and warmth in his voice.

"I cannot learn to love others until I learn to love myself. I cannot overcome hatred until I have mastered love. Today I will love more deeply and will allow myself to demonstrate my love of all mankind. I will learn to labor in love and serve and love myself and all others - especially those who hate me."

After Gerard spoke these words, the dragon quickly shrank to the size of a mouse and ran off into a sewer drain along the west side of the castle.

The dragon of ignorance reared its ugly head and quickly morphed itself into a man. It transformed into the form of Marlo the Magnificent - the greatest and most beloved knight in all the land.

"What just happened? Why is Marlo the Magnificent here? Is he a dragon in disguise?" Gerard's head was spinning.

"Our young and noble knight," Sir Tristan and Garland spoke simultaneously, "there are many dragons in disguise all around us. Some are very cunning and very attractive because they appear to be of value when all they do is devalue you. If you look to others and try to follow their examples, especially when they walk down erring paths, then you are being led by the dragons of ignorance. This can also happen when you believe that dragons are only in the shape of dragons. Danger surrounds you at every step in your journey through life. You must continually be on the lookout for dragons and demons that seek to destroy you, for they are everywhere. Have faith in yourself and believe that you have great intelligence, for you do. You can think your way out of any problem or disaster that befalls you. You must use your intelligence to think your way out of the clutches of this deadly dragon."

"I must think my way out of this using *my* intelligence," thought Gerard to himself. After repeating this a few times, Knight Gerard looked up and said:

"I have always thought I was an intelligent person and could foresee problems that befell me and quickly surmise solutions, but I could never have foreseen these problems. I do believe in myself and I do have faith in myself and also faith in Sir Tristan the Great and Garland the Invisible. They would not lead me astray. They will not forsake me. I must face you for myself, as myself. You are my dragon and you are part of me. Could it be that if I put my faith and trust in those who are undeserving of it and those who try to lead me astray that I will not be true to who I am? Sir Tristan the Great and Garland the Invisible have continually referred to me as a noble knight. I have not always been as noble as I should have been, but starting now I will be. Nobility is my birthright and I will no longer follow in the shadows of ignorance. I must think for myself and think how my thoughts, words, and actions affect myself and others. The effects can be severe and destructive for myself and others. I choose, this day and always, to be a knight of nobility!"

And with those simple yet powerful words, the dragon of Marlo the Magnificent vanished. Sir Tristan the Great and Garland the Invisible appeared and congratulated Knight Gerard.

"Now you have proven yourself to yourself. You have defeated the dragons for today, but these dragons and many more will continue to haunt you every day. You must bravely face them each day and as you do so, you will have greater happiness and strength. Greet each day with love and you will be blessed with happiness." Sir Tristan finished and smiled.

"I will strive daily to be a knight of nobility," said Knight Gerard! And with that the three brave knights opened the castle drawbridge as the sun began to rise on a new day! It was beautiful, filled with hope and possibility. Knight Gerard now knew that he was not alone and had learned to believe in himself and the love of those around him.

The Wealthy Businessman

Garret Matheson, was a wealthy businessman who had amassed a great fortune during his lifetime creating profitable companies and products that were not only practical and necessary, but were affordable and well built. He was somewhat of an inventor and had several patents. Garret believed that the truly successful businesses were the ones who retained the rights and ownership of their products. He had a very large business empire and, unfortunately, three very greedy and ungrateful sons. One day he called all three sons into his office.

"I want to let each of you know I am not giving any of you anything as an inheritance - not one dime! I feel inheritances corrupt good, promising men. It degrades and devalues them because they soon come to depend on and expect what they feel they are entitled to because of their birth. Most men and women who receive an inheritance or win the lottery quickly lose their money because they have never learned how to earn income, save it and in a similar manner invest it wisely. Everything I have acquired in life has come about because of hard work, sacrifice, and commitment to a cause - being dedicated and serving others. I want each of you to be as committed to your own cause. I want you to learn how to sacrifice, serve, work hard, and honestly earn your own fortunes. As of today, I will not financially back or support any of you. You must prove yourselves to me and to yourselves. From this day forward you are financially responsible for yourselves."

The three brothers were shocked and devastated by the news. The two oldest were even outraged.

"You want us to get a job?" the oldest brother scowled

defiantly.

"My sons, I have done you all a great disservice. I did not teach you to work. When you were younger I should have taught you to appreciate work, to take pride in the work you do, to be responsible, and accountable. You are all grown men in your 20s. When I was in my late 20s I was already married with one child and working two jobs to pay the bills, while creating my first company on the side, working late into the evenings and on the weekends. This is how I began and how you will as well.

"I want to let each of you know I am firm about not giving any of you anything as an inheritance. In the future, when I have left this world behind, I will be dividing my estate and I hope to entrust everything to the three of you to help oversee the charitable donations, and proper distribution of our family trust funds. I hope we will leave a legacy of serving and helping others by using our finances to build up communities and bless the lives of many."

Garret quickly left his three bewildered sons and began preparing a unique test for each of them. Each of these tests would be personalized and set up to focus on each son's strengths and weaknesses. If they could pass the first test then they would be allowed to prove themselves over the next two years. They would then all need to live on their own and provide for themselves.

A few days went by and the three sons were called into their father's office to be interviewed.

"What are you going to do, quiz us on what it means to be successful?," questioned Drake, the oldest son.

"No, my son, it will be much more than that. I am not having any of you take a multiple choice test, a quiz, write out an essay, or anything of the kind. My test will be much better, more difficult, and more enlightening for you and me. Your first test, that each of you must perform, is to give everything you own away to those who really need it."

"You can't be serious, Dad!?," Bradley, the youngest son, began. "You mean everything we own?"

"That's right," quipped the father. "I mean everything. Even every gift you ever received growing up - everything. None of you has ever had a job before so you have never purchased anything with your own hard earned money. All of your clothes, books, games, technology, toys, and even the cars we gave each of you for your 21st birthdays - give everything away! Give it *all* away." The wealthy businessman was not joking and looked at each of them with hope and simply whispered, "Now get to work!"

"You want us to give away all our clothes?" Kyle, the middle son could barely utter the words. He, more than his two brothers, loved fashion and always wore the best and most expensive imported clothing from the finest designers around the world.

"That's right," Garret began, "but I will allow each of you to keep one outfit - pick your very favorite outfit and give the rest away. No exceptions. Don't even keep one extra shirt, suit, or scarf. Give everything away to someone who needs it more than you."

"But how can we survive with only one outfit?" Once again, Kyle shrieked his disapproval.

"Kyle, you can have all the outfits you want, as long as *you* buy them yourself. You see, I purchased all of these outfits with my own money. You are free to do whatever you want with the money you earn because that would be your money - not mine. But remember, you don't have a cent to your name. With your taste in designer clothing and name brands, it may take you awhile before you can afford to purchase what you enjoy wearing." The father looked at each of his sons and smiled kindly. "I am doing all of you a great favor and am drastically improving the quality of your lives right now as we speak. You may not enjoy any of this or appreciate what is happening, but this will help you become men - men I can be proud of and more important, men *you* can be proud of. Now quickly go and do what I have asked of you. You don't have much time to waste." And with that, the sons left the room, shaking their confused heads and angrily arguing about their future.

It was a very difficult task asked of the sons. They all did as they were asked and each felt empty and lost without their possessions. Kyle felt the most betrayed and was the most bitter of all the brothers.

After having completed their father's wishes, the sons understandably felt confused and unsure about everything.

"Why would dad force us to give away everything we own. Yes, he purchased everything with his money, but it all belonged to us." Kyle could not hide his anger and frustration. The three brothers met back in their father's home office, a grand and spacious room that intimidated even the most prominent business people.

"Please come in and meet with me one at a time so I may tell you what I expect of you individually and so you may freely speak to me one on one." Garret looked at each of his sons and then continued.

"Let's start with the oldest and work our way down. Please come in, Drake."

Drake was the most athletic of the three boys. He always loved playing sports and especially enjoyed all water sports. One of his favorite activities was boating.

"Drake, my son, you are the oldest and as such, have

a great responsibility. The other two boys look up to you. You are all old enough to be called men, but I believe you earn the title of being a man. You don't simply come of age because a calendar proclaims the arrival of your birthday. It is time for you to truly become a man."

"I don't agree with anything you are doing, father, but I do respect you." Drake looked down at the floor as if he were a little boy again.

"I'm glad you respect me, son. Respect is gained with great difficulty over many years and can be lost in a matter of a few seconds by foolish choices that seem important at the time. I don't want you to waste away your life playing in the water." Garret stood up from his office chair and came to the front of his beautiful mahogany desk and sat on it.

"I don't think I am wasting away my life at all." Drake's protest sounded more profound when he had said it quietly to himself before erupting and letting his words spew out of his mouth.

"Son, there is nothing wrong with having fun. Life should be fun. The problem is when you only focus on the fun and don't work at all. Now I think you should have fun with your work because if you don't absolutely love what you do each day, you will be very miserable very quickly in life. I want you to have fun, but that fun is more meaningful when you make sure that what you are doing is providing meaningful and enjoyable entertainment or education for others. If you can create that then you will be able to create a sustainable lifestyle where others will gladly trade their hard earned money for what you are offering them. You will be able to provide for yourself."

"I want to," replied Drake, "I just don't know how to be profitable."

"You can be profitable in anything if you work at it and

help set others up for success, fun, excitement, or simply having a good time. Here's an idea - what if you created a company of your own that focused on how much fun individuals and families can have being together. Play together and stay together. It could be in the water, on boats, camping, climbing, or any other outdoor activity you create." Garret looked his son in the eyes and then continued.

"This is what I want you to do. I will appoint you as a lower level associate in my real estate company, one of the branches of my various business ventures, and will begin paying you an hourly wage. Once you demonstrate you can handle that for a few months, or sooner if you increase your work load and capacity, then I will begin to give you more responsibilities until you are a salaried employee. During that time these are the two things I want you to do. First, I want you to create a company of your own. Come up with a company name, a business plan, what products or services you will market to your customers, and then research who your customers would be. Second, after two years as one of my employees, I am going to fire you. I'm giving you ample forewarning so you can be prepared. During those two years, I will work with you on your business plan and help you create your first company. You will be responsible for finding investors to fund your company, however..."

"Wait a minute," interjected Drake. "You want me to work for you only so you can fire me and then on top of that you want me to create my own company and find investors of my own? What about you? Why can't you fund my company?"

"I can fund your company as any other investor would, but I will take a percentage of your company. Is that what you want? I could also give you a loan but there would be interest charged to the loan. Would that work instead?"

"What would be the point of that?," asked Drake. "I may as well do it myself if you would need ownership of the company and won't give it to me for free."

"Great! But nothing is free Drake. I know you are kidding, but I am not. If you will invest in yourself and your own ability, you will be very successful. You will then have the opportunity to be your own boss, and will have a greater sense of satisfaction because you'll have done the work on your own. Let's start today. I will pay you $15 an hour which is a very reasonable rate of employment seeing as how you don't really have any skills or education in any certain field and absolutely no work experience. If you can work hard enough and prove yourself to me and to yourself, I will then raise your hourly rate to $25 per hour. I will only do that, of course, when you demonstrate to me your dependability, accountability, and your actual ability to learn how to do what is required of the job. Oh, and by the way, you will work at least 40 hours a week every week. Shall we shake on it and you can start your new job tomorrow, if you'd like?"

Drake looked at his father, rolled his eyes and laughed out loud.

"You're kidding, right? $15 dollars an hour working for you for 40 hours straight every week. That's $600 dollars per week. That equals $2,400 per month. I can't live on that!" Drake's laughter stopped and a frown came over his face when he realized his father was not joking at all.

"Well son, that's $2,400 per month before taxes. Remember that taxes will be taken out and you will need to get your own health insurance plan because I will no longer be covering your health insurance. Also, you won't be living here any more. I'm sorry but you need to make your own way in the world so you will need to find somewhere else to live. You are wearing everything you own so you won't be taking anything with you anyway. If you need to get around town, and you will because you will need to have some transportation for work, you will need to get a car. Once you have a car, you will need car insurance. Thankfully you are not married yet and don't have a family, so you will not need any life insurance. If something happened to you I could cover the expenses for a casket, burial spot, etc.. This way, you can focus more on your work and getting everything in place for creating a business plan for your own business you'd like to create."

Drake was completely shocked. His jaw dropped as his father continued.

"You'll also need to use some of the money for a place to rent. You don't have enough money to buy a house and you don't have anything for a down-payment anyway. It's getting to be more expensive every day. If you'd like, I can have you stay in one of my rental properties I own and we can deduct the monthly rent and living expenses from your paycheck. That might make it easier for you and me since I recently have had trouble getting renters in a few of my units. Please send both of your brothers in and I will speak to them at the same time. I will share with them everything I have shared with you. The only difference will be in what I am having each of you do. You all will have two years to begin thinking about what you would like to do with the rest of your life. Think of this as a wonderful gift you are being given to really live life on your own with no strings attached. Since you will be on your own, you can decide what you will do with your time. You will, of course, pay everything with your own dime. As long as you show up to work everyday and do a great job, you won't have to worry about losing your employment and seeking new employment anytime soon."

And with that, the wealthy businessman dismissed his oldest son and met with the other two. In speaking with his next oldest and youngest sons, he shared the same information, advice, and plan for their next two years. The only difference was that Kyle would be employed in one of his factories, and Bradley would work for a book publishing company of which Garret was part owner and would soon acquire complete ownership. All three of the sons moved out and began working. It was, to them, the most horrible day of their short-lived 20 something years on earth.

The next few weeks were the most challenging for all three of the sons. Each had their own weaknesses and shortcomings, and each had so much to learn. To make sure his sons were treated equally among his other employees and to see to it they did not receive any special treatment or privileges, he kept their identity hidden. Only a few people knew who his sons really were. He had told each of his sons that they would be fined $1,000 dollars for each time they told a co-worker who they really were.

After a few months of learning their various duties and responsibilities, each son began gaining confidence in what he did and what he might do in the future. They had learned how to budget and even started saving a little money. All three of the sons had to take out loans to get a car. Garret had contacted all of the local dealerships and told them they could not sell anything to his sons that cost more than $5,000. The sons could not use their father as collateral and the wealthy businessman wanted the car dealerships to know it. Each son began to not only work harder than they ever had, but each son genuinely began to love the work they were doing. Each son also found that they had a natural talent for filling the responsibilities in the various positions. Little did they know that their father, Garret, had selected each of the various companies and positions for his sons after reviewing their strengths and weaknesses.

Another six months flew by and the sons began to lead out in their individual positions at work.

Because of the many successes each son had, they all received a raise and were each making $25 dollars per hour. Each son began arriving at work a little earlier and even staying a little later. The three sons became driven to work harder and accomplish more. They now knew what it felt like to have small successes for work well done and all three began to want more of that feeling. As they worked harder and did more the father was pleased with their diligence and ability to work hard. But one day, after about 10 months into their two year agreement, Garret called his three sons into a meeting with him. He sat at one end of the table and his three sons sat at the other. No one spoke for the first few minutes and then the father said,

"My boys, I am delighted with the work you are doing. It is impressive and each of you are excelling as I hoped you would. My only complaint is that you must find time to live life as well. Work is wonderful and is good, but if that is all you do, then you will not live a life worth living. You see, if you truly enjoy what you do it will not seem like work to you because you love it and it becomes part of you. Then each morning becomes a joy because you can't wait to wake up and go to work. The excitement of all you will accomplish that day becomes a beautiful blessing in your life. It is not a curse, but a cause worth pursuing. However, if that is all you see in your horizon, then you will live a sad and lonely life."

"There is more to life than work," Garret continued. "Much more. From now on I want you to only work 30 hours per week but find a way to make the same amount of income that you had when you were working 40 hours per week. It will take some creative thinking and you will need to start thinking like a businessman, but every month from now on I will have you work less hours per week and at the same time continue to earn the same fixed amount of money you are earning now. If you can even earn more than you are earning now while continuing to work fewer hours, than you presently are, then all the better. This is your challenge. Good luck, my sons!"

And with that Garret dismissed his three sons and told them they could ask him any questions on their own individually.

At first, the three sons were confused. They each had grown accustomed to working 40 plus hours per week and truly enjoyed doing their work. How could they possibly cut back their hours and work less while still earning the same amount of income? It didn't seem logical.

The youngest son, Bradley, had an innovative idea that he thought would help him accomplish what his father was asking him to do and asked to meet with his father.

"Is there any way we can try something out and see if it will work for me?" Bradley asked.

"I'm listening, son. What do you have in mind?"

"I have been going over my position at the book publishing department and believe I can spend five hours per week doing what I am doing if I hire someone to take my place and handle the more time consuming aspects of my job. The rest I will handle myself. Currently you are paying me around $25 dollars per hour plus bonuses when we land accounts and finalize various publishing deals and contracts with authors and photographers. I believe I can hire someone who can do those tasks that will take the burden and time away from me. If we pay him or her

$15 dollars per hour to begin with, and If I can keep the remaining $10 dollars per hour to find other ways to help the staff become more entrepreneurially minded, then I believe I can generate additional income to possibly exceed what I am currently making each month."

Bradley looked over at his father to see his reaction and hoped his father would agree to his plan.

"I like where your mind is going. It's a shift in perspective where you are thinking more like an entrepreneur and less like an employee. That is a very important transition. You cannot have your own company unless you begin to think outside of the box and focus more on creating residual based products or services that afford you more free time to pursue other interests." The wealthy businessman allowed a tiny smile to creep across his face. He then continued, "But how do you propose we encourage the other employees to become more entrepreneurially minded? Most want to remain employees and would never do more than they were asked to do. Don't you think?"

"I think I have an idea of how to begin creating residual income for myself as well as helping others, even those who only want to remain as employees. If you will go along with it, I'd love to start trying some of these ideas. I think it will only help the company do better."

"I'm listening, son. What are your ideas? Have you thought this through? Do you have a plan?"

"It isn't a concrete plan yet, father, but I have an idea and would love to run it by you. This is what I have thought. Ultimately I would love to write my own books in the future - but that is only for my benefit. I have always had a passion for writing and feel that I could excel if I pushed myself in that direction. I know the publishing industry has changed and isn't what is was even a few years ago. With that being said, I feel I have learned a great deal to help me in coming out with my own books in the future. Second, I think all of the employees have great ideas and can be even more successful than they currently are. A few months ago you gave me a bonus because of a new shipping supplier company I had contacted and convinced to be our only supplier of shipping supplies. The prices for the containers were much lower and the savings has added so much to our bottom line. The way I see it, we can either increase our business capacity with new clients and customers, or we can decrease our expenses and both will help us be more profitable and grow as a company."

"That is all true, but how does that help the other employees and how does this information help you personally to create residual income?" Always one to keep his youngest son on track and focused, Garret motioned for his son to continue and get to the point.

"You see, father, I found out from another employee about that shipping supply company. I did all of the contacting and finalized the deal, but would never have known about the company without this recommendation from a fellow employee. You then gave me a $1,000 dollar bonus that month. Because I had received the information from this other co-worker, I split the bonus with him. He was ecstatic and began offering great insight and suggestions that have truly helped our company. It was as if he came alive! I believe that we need to have a training seminar once a month for each of our employees to help encourage them to improve and become better employees. We will teach them how to take initiative and do more than they are asked to do in their daily employee responsibilities. Every employee can also be given advice, motivation, and will be taught tools on how to receive more training and will then be of more value to the company."

"I like what you are suggesting. I assume you will want

to help train these employees, correct? And be paid?"

"Yes, father. I suggest we offer two 1-2 hour long training sessions every two weeks. There will be only two per month, and I think we could offer the first two as free training for everyone. I suggest after that, the employees will need to pay $10 dollars every two weeks for a combined total of $20 dollars per month per employee. In these training sessions I would like to demonstrate to the employees how they can receive a percentage of the bonus that is handed out for landing new accounts. Generally speaking, it has only ever gone to managers. What if the individual who makes the suggestion or comes up with the idea is compensated if a new client signs up or if they help us in our daily decision making process. That way everyone will feel as if they have a stake in the company. What are your thoughts, dad?"

Garret thought about it for a moment and then said, "I think it is a wonderful idea, but I don't know that you would have very many employees who would want to pay $20 dollars per month. Maybe 10% at the most, if that, and there are only 140 employees in this publishing company. You would likely only have 14 or so who would want to pay the $20 dollars per month which only gives you an extra $280 dollars per month. That is not very much residual, son. It's a start, but not much."

"Father, I had thought about that. I think the employees should not pay for the seminars outright, so to speak. I think it should be deducted from their monthly paycheck. In addition to that, I was hoping I could do these seminars for all of your employees in all of your companies. I realized that only about 10% or so would want to do it and we can't force anyone to do it, but you currently have almost 4,500 employees working in all of your various companies. That would be 450 employees if only 10%

attended the monthly seminars. If we multiply that number by $20 dollars per employee, we end up with $9,000 dollars per month. For setting up the seminars and teaching the employees how they can increase their personal profits by becoming more entrepreneurial in their thinking, I would ask for $4,000 dollars of the $9,000. You can keep and then turn around and re-invest the remaining $5,000 into your various companies because that would be $5,000 less you would be paying your employees each month."

The father was impressed by this idea his son had.

"Essentially, son, you would be teaching them skills to be more productive and help the company be more profitable. What if you motivate employees we have to leave my companies and be successful somewhere else."

"I think that should be part of our focus as well to help each employee know that we want them to succeed - if not with us and our company, then somewhere else. We could even create cross job applications from one of your companies to each of the others. If the employees are not happy in your book publishing company they might succeed and enjoy working in your real-estate company. We can teach them that we have their best interest in mind and want them to grow and receive more training, certifications, skills, etc.. If the employees know that we will help them find their dream job, then I believe we can and will have many new applicants who want to join the company family. These company seminars can be thought of as mastermind groups where we encourage them to follow their dreams and succeed. I know it may take awhile for the idea to catch on within the company, but I would like to try. For that purpose I would like to do a month or even two for free. I would like to create resources that can be purchased by the employees as well to help increase my monthly income."

Bradley stopped speaking and looked at his father

for guidance and direction. Garret placed his hands on his son's shoulders and said, "Now you are thinking like a businessman. It is not about the time it takes to create the company and product. It is about creating a system, making sure it works, and is valuable to your intended market, and then helping your ideas succeed and improve. Let me ask you, are my companies the only ones you would like to visit and help train?"

"No. I would like to begin visiting several other local companies in the city and offering them this service as well after we have successfully tried the company and the seminars out on the employees in your companies. I have spoken with many of the current employees within the book publishing company and they all feel that they would like to know how they can increase their chances for a raise or a bonus here and there. I have already created a 30 page PDF handout I'd like to show you that outlines what I would like to teach and focus on in a step by step procedure for helping the employees become more profitable. If they can see the value in advancing their careers and improving their own lives, then I think they will willingly attend these bi-weekly mastermind meetings. Their success will help my success become a reality. We can all win together as we learn and grow."

After hearing this from his youngest son, Garret was excited for him to try out his idea. Until you put an idea forward you never know how it will turn out. As it happened, initially, about 250 employees from all of the companies committed to attending the mastermind meetings every two weeks. Bradley began teaching the hopeful employees from the various companies and would teach them about changing their outlook on what they were doing and why they were doing it. As a result of these meetings, more and more of the employees began arriving earlier, staying a little later at times, and doing more than was outlined in their job description. The majority of those who attended these two monthly mastermind sessions improved not only their productivity as employees, but each contributed to the overall prosperity of the company. This in turn brought raises and bonuses to these employees. After six months of teaching these mastermind meetings for the employees, word quickly spread and more employees from within Garret's companies began attending. Each knew they would learn skills to increase their own abilities which increased their dependability and capability. This also increased their own marketability and personal profitability in addition to the improved profitability of the company.

In seeing their younger brother's success, the older brothers began counseling with him and asking him for advice as well as visiting with their father for ideas. Within a year all three brothers had created companies of their own and were gradually building their own ventures and investing in themselves. Their father, the wealthy businessman, had said the best advice he could give any of them would be to invest in themselves, their ideas, their thinking, knowledge, talents, skills, abilities, etc.. By learning and growing and creating something, the brothers began to trust in their own ideas. Each began creating their own dream maps and began actively pursuing what they wanted to accomplish.

Garret knew that until his three sons learned to think for themselves, work for themselves, and try to create companies of their own, they would never truly live life, because they would continually depend on their father and his ability. He wanted his sons to achieve and accomplish results for themselves and learn to think things through, come up with solutions to their own problems, and determine how to truly *live* life!

The Island of "I CAN" and the Isle of "I CAN'T"

In a not too distant part of the world there was a big island, and a little beyond the island was a small isle. Both lands were beautiful. Both lands were abundant with natural resources and both lands were inhabited with people.

On the big island, the people were very productive and active. They never wasted their time or complained about the work they did. Everyone was very successful and accomplished so much. In addition to the great success of the people on the big island, they also had many hobbies, interests, and wonderful experiences. They lived life to its fullest. Their world was bright, beautiful, and a blessing because of their optimistic outlook on life.

Everyone on the big island believed and knew they could accomplish anything they set out to accomplish and knew they could become anyone they wanted to become. They all believed in themselves. The island was known as the island of "I CAN".

The little isle beyond the island, however, became known as the isle of "I CAN'T" because of the negativity of the people who lived there. They, unfortunately, were not productive at all and thought they would fail if they attempted to do something they had never done before. As a result of this thinking, no one did anything because they would not challenge themselves and push the limits of possibility. To them, everything was impossible.

The inhabitants on the isle of "I CAN'T" were extremely jealous with everyone on the island of "I CAN". They would often complain about how unjust it was and how the people on the island of "I CAN" had an unfair advantage over the people on the isle of "I CAN'T". "I'm sure," they would often say, "that if I lived on the island of 'I CAN', I would be very productive and extremely successful. Despite their complaints, no one ever suggested a plan that would help the people of "I

143

CANT."

One bright and beautiful day, one of the islanders from the island of "I CAN" said, "I think we could send some of our "I can" people to the isle of "I CAN'T" to help them. Everyone on the island of "I CAN" was excited. They genuinely wanted to help out the people of "I CAN'T". Someone from the isle of "I CAN'T" found out and said, "If people from the island of "I CAN" are coming to our little isle, then we need to send people to their island as well - it's only fair. Besides, if we live on the island of 'I CAN' for a period of time, we will be as productive and prosperous as they are."

It was agreed - a group of families, men, women, teens, and children from both the "I CAN" island and the isle of "I CAN'T" traded places. It was an adventure! Now there were "I Can" islanders on the isle of "I CAN'T" and there were also "I Can't" individuals on the island of "I CAN". Both groups decided to remain in their new area for two years and then return and see how the groups were doing.

Two years later came sooner than either party had expected and so they decided to return and report of their activities.

The individuals originally from the isle of "I CAN'T" sadly said life was as unproductive and unsuccessful on the island of "I CAN" as it had been for them before on their own isle. At first, they felt as if they could change when they saw how excited and engaged the islanders were on the island of "I CAN." "They make everything look easy on the island, but it's not! We can't do what they can and we also can't stand how positive and optimistic everyone is. They honestly think they can do anything they put their mind to - simply by believing they can and then doing it", one of the "I Can't" individuals said.

Next, one of the "I CAN" islanders spoke up.

"These last two years have been more productive and rewarding for us. We have accomplished so much and are so amazed at the overwhelming opportunities on the isle of 'I CAN'T'. In fact, we have had so much success working with the children and the youth and helped so many of them realize they can do anything they put their mind to. When we first arrived on the isle we heard nothing but negativity, pessimism, and complaints about what we hoped to accomplish. They all murmured that we wouldn't be able to accomplish anything worthwhile or productive while on their isle. At first, some of our "I CAN" people were saddened and pained by their negative comments and some were momentarily downcast and felt despair - but that didn't last for very long. We went to work and began doing things. Several of the children and teenagers had never done any work in their lives and most didn't think they could do anything because they were all told they are "I Can't" individuals and that they can't be successful or won't amount to much so they shouldn't even bother trying. We told them that kind of thinking was wrong."

"How dare you corrupt our youth and teach them they can do anything they believe they can!" Yelled one of the "I Can't" men.

"We showed the children and the youth that we believed in them and gave them a little encouragement. That was all they needed. It really didn't take very much or very long before we were surrounded by many "I Can" attitudes. It was wonderful to see the change and know that they can do anything if they believe they can. The majority of the adults are still as negative as they were before, but we have hope for the rising generation."

Both parties debated for some time about how effective or ineffective the exchange had been and both parties decided to continue living their lives as they had before.

What did change on the island of "I CAN" and on the isle of "I CAN'T" were the children and the teenagers. Many, but not all, of the children and teenagers on the isle of "I CAN'T" began to believe, for the first time, in themselves. They began to think and say "I can" and it slowly began to make a difference on the isle. More and more "I CAN" attitudes were being cultivated and developed on the isle of "I CAN'T". Many became very productive because of their hard work and positive belief and many were very successful in most everything they did - because they believed they could.

Unfortunately, the same effect had happened on the island of "I CAN". Many of the children and teenagers were negatively affected by the "I CAN'T" visitors who had told them for almost two years straight that they couldn't and wouldn't be successful or productive in life. They discouraged the children and teens so much from setting goals and actively participating in life, that many of the youth began to believe the lies they heard. They felt they weren't good enough, smart enough, pretty enough, or capable enough to accomplish anything and many - far too many - began to lose interest in doing their best and being their best. Some didn't try because they believed they would make mistakes and fail. Before the two year trade, everyone on the island of "I CAN" had encouraged the children, teenagers, and adults to actively try and not to worry about making mistakes or perceived failures. Everyone knew they were only stepping stones to true success. That of course had changed.

Now both the island of "I CAN" and the isle of "I CAN'T" had "I can" attitudes and "I can't" beliefs as well. Both perspectives were prevalent. Both groups of people were trying to co-exist and work together. The "I Can's" and the "I Cant's" are both correct. They can and cannot do whatever they believe they can and cannot do.

Malcus's Tale

Once upon a time, in a far off distant land - but not too distant past, there lived a great king in a grand castle. He ruled the land by honesty and asked his family, children, neighbors, and all the members of his house and kingdom to strictly observe and follow two rules: first, to be obedient, and second, to be completely honest in everything they did.

"You see," said he, "Honesty is not the best policy, it is the only policy." He then continued, "I urge you to be honest in everything you do and in everything you say. Be honest to yourselves. Be honest to your spouse and children, to your parents, and siblings. If you are honest in your dealings with your fellow men, you will never need to explain yourself or justify any action you do, because you would never do or say anything dishonest or questionable in the first place. In doing so, you are also being obedient. Obey the laws of the land. Children obey your parents. Parents obey the lessons you learned as children, for I and my father, the noble king who served you in your youth, have taught each of you and your families the correct way to lead fulfilling lives of integrity, virtue, righteousness, personal prosperity, and spiritual sanctity. My people—be honest and obedient to God, for He is the King of kings. Observe and diligently follow all of His commandments, do His will, and His work. Pray to Him, and follow Him. He loves you and I love you. Please serve each other. Share your talents with others and enrich the lives of everyone with whom you interact that they may know of the goodness of the God you follow. You will be richly blessed in life if you are honest and obedient. It doesn't matter what others believe, say, or do—always do what you know is true!

147

"You will be blessed for your obedience to God. Everything you have and everything you are is a gift from God. Your gift to Him is your obedience and your willingness to do whatever He asks of you. I ask of you to pledge your allegiance to the almighty King of kings. Give everything you are to the giver of all gifts - your eternal Father in Heaven. He is GOOD. HE *is* GOD. "

After hearing their king speak in such a way, the people happily decided they would be completely obedient and honest at all times. Everyone, that is, except for one short, stubborn little man named Malcus. Malcus did not want anyone to tell him what he could and could not do. He thought it childish to follow rules and do anything that was not self serving or self gratifying. He was a little self-absorbed, very selfish, and at times, even self-righteous. He thought he knew best and that others should do things his way, even if they weren't according to the wishes of the king, his fellow men, or even God. He decided to ignore the admonishing plea from the good king. He thought it was more beneficial for everyone to be a little dishonest here and there. It may not have been favorable for everyone, but being a little dishonest did help him do better in business and he thought he wouldn't be able to earn as much, or have the kind of lifestyle he thought he should have, if he were completely honest. He also thought it silly to pray to someone he thought didn't exist and had never blessed his life before anyway.

Days and months and years went on, as they always do, and Malcus became more disobedient, dishonest, and dissatisfied with life. His dishonesty and disobedience had brought upon him natural consequences, as they always do, which were not self serving, and which eventually became self-destructive. He thought his family, his neighbors, his king, and the God he didn't believe existed were abandoning him. It was his choice to disobey and be dishonest. Yet, at the time, rarely does anyone see the perilous problems and potential pains that their daily decisions will bring them at some future time. In a last attempt to plead his case and his cause to anyone who would listen, he journeyed to the grand castle to meet with the great king.

The great king graciously accepted him into his celestial-like castle and asked how he could serve Malcus and better help him. Malcus blatantly blamed his family, his neighbors, and even the king and the God he didn't believe existed for making his life so miserable. He blamed everyone — except himself.

"I have nothing but pain, sorrow, frustration, worry, and endless suffering each and every day of my life," Malcus began. He then continued, "I am the only one who has all these misfortunes, struggles, tragedies, disappointments, and problems in life. No one knows how difficult my life is. Everyone has left me and I am now all alone."

The great king thought for some time before speaking. He could easily have chided the man for his stubbornness and inability to follow two simple rules, be obedient and be honest, and that the man had brought all of this upon himself because of the choices he had made in life, but instead, the great king said, "God understands and knows you." The king then continued, "No one is perfect and everyone struggles on a daily basis, but when we put our faith in God, He strengthens us and He blesses us to meet the challenges of the day. We pray for His help and His ability to guide us on our journey through life, but we must travel through life's trials and face them with His assistance. Alone, we can do nothing, but with God all things are possible because He is our Father and we are

His children.

With tears streaming down his face, Malcus nodded, and for the first time, in a very long time, Malcus apologized. He then said, "What can I do to change?" The king whispered his reply, "Malcus let us obey God and honestly live the lives He wants us to live. Let us put God first, and everything else will work itself out. As we put our faith in our Father in Heaven, He guides us down the paths that lead to eternal happiness—in His presence—home again in the celestial courts above."

Malcus smiled, and he and the great king embraced and vowed to both put their trust in the King of all kings - in God, the eternal father.

Fearless and Wreckless

One young sailor set out to sail the seas. He was adventurous, brave, and fearless, but he was sometimes careless, reckless, and heartless. He thought he would conquer the world. He thought he could command the sea to take him where he wanted to go and to see what he wanted to see.

Sadly, the young sailor and his shipmates shipwrecked. Every sailor abandoned ship and began to fend for himself. There was no comradery. They were no longer united in one dream to sail the seven seas. Each man looked out for himself and his own interests. They each went their separate ways. The entire crew, including the adventurous young sailor, disappeared and were never heard from again. It was believed they all drowned because they would not work together to save each other. If they had helped each other and truly been united as a crew ought to be, they might have lived to tell the tale and sail the seven seas again.

Me, Myself, and I

The simpleton met a pimpleton,
pampered by pomp and pride.
Consumed by himself,
infatuated by his eye,
seeking the approval of each passerby.

We refer to this creature as
"Me, Myself, and I" -
telling us all everything that he knows,
proclaiming perfection while his ego grows.

Every conversation centers on himself,
he prays that the world will praise him.
He's like a product sitting on the shelf,
always selling his features, his color, and size,
seeking acclamation from the beholder's eyes.

"Me, Myself, and I,"
consumed with my wants and needs -
looking out for myself,
doing what I please,
disregarding all else except for *my* deeds.

Is it a wonder this beast consumes itself?
Feeds it's ego and dines with itself?
Baby's and pampers its' repugnant pride,
and fears rejection and tries to hide -
from humility, and responsibility?
Is it any wonder at all?

"Me myself, and I,"
what a terrible creature
what a horrid beast,
I think it will devour itself as its' feast.

The Chasm that Divides

The broken bridge needed some mending,
no one dared cross it at all.
For the chasm that divided the two separate sides
would inevitably cause people to fall.

There were treasures and wonders on the other side,
dreams would come true when there.
But in front of the chasm that divided the two sides,
was a sign that warned "Beware!"

"Steer clear of this path!
Some may succeed, but most will fail,
and this chasm was created to divide you in two.
The ones who do and the others who don't,
the ones who accomplish and the others who won't.

"Only the determined will make it across,
all others will quit and give up.
But if you dream of doing things,
and if you relentlessly toil,
you'll have crossed the chasm that divides these two sides,
and will end up on prosperous soil."

The Flowers in My Garden

The flowers in my garden,
have many names - and yet,
each flower in my garden,
was planted, at first, in regret -

Regret for the garden I used to have,
for the flowers that once were mine -
regret for the beauty that lived and died,
and the flowers I've left behind.

The Candle Burned Brightly

The candle burned brightly,
it flickered and grew.
The wind bellowed loudly,
it blew and blew.

The wind tried to blow
the little light out.
But the candle burned brighter
and so the wind tried to shout.

He shouted and screamed,
he wailed and moaned,
but that little light grew
every time the wind blew.

When the winds wail and mourn
and there arises a terrible storm,
does our light grow brighter
or does it grow darker and forlorn?

The OneSuchHere and The NoneSuchHere

I went to the land of NoneSuchHere
to see if any dreamers dwelt there.
And their reply, was one of those who didn't care:
"In this town are NoneSuchHere."

In that same town of NoneSuchHere
a dreamer arrived and then resided there.
And to the NoneSuchHere he proclaimed:
"In this town is OneSuchHere."

Each NoneSuch turned to this OneSuch and asked
"How do we help such dreams appear?"
The OneSuch told the NoneSuch there,
"Let faith overpower whatever you fear.

"Faith can work miracles,
moving mountains, and rivers, and seas -
doing all that you want and ask it to -
faith works for the one who believes."

And in that land of NoneSuchHere
faith grew and soon overpowered fear.
Then in that town, hundreds of OneSuchHeres
began succeeding and eliminating their fears.

Each OneSuch helped each Nonesuch there
to dream and plan and conquer their fear.

In your town is there OneSuchHere?,
who will show the rest how to conquer their fear?

How Starfish Came to Be

I found a little star,
that had fallen from the sky.
He lost his light and cried that he,
never again would brilliant be.

This little star sobbed and cried for days
until the moon called out one starry night,
and said, "My friend,
I think you've lost your light."

"Why do you cry and mourn like this?
What do these sad sobs mean?
Could it be you've given up on yourself,
on your hopes, on your plans, on your dream?"

"Wise moon in the sky,
I'll tell you why, I sob and wail and cry.
I once was brilliant all eyes looked to me,
then I fell from the sky and now never can be,
a guiding light to those who look up
hoping to see a shooting star,
beaming from Heaven, so near, so far.
I can never return - I only look up
and see what I can never again be."

"Little star, it's true, you can never return
to the sky from whence you came.
But you are a star, that never will change,
your value will always remain.

"I've seen many stars fall from the sky,
and each star always wonders why.
So I tell them each to remember their worth,
and bring smiles to children who live here on earth.

"You've fallen in a special place,
on the shore, beside the sea.
And children are always searching
for the treasures they hope they'll see.

"Stay where you are, do not hide away.
Listen for children's laughter.
Look at their smiles and see them play,
it's you they'll all be after.

"When the children pick you up
and hold you in their hands,
you'll feel again the light,
but not from heavenly lands.

"These children share their light as love,
they smile and laugh and play.
And to some you're thought a *star fish*,
but to children, you light up their day."

Men Must Work

The men who work the hardest, I find,
are the men who are committed to the work they do.
And sadly, beginners are many,
and enders are often few,
because they fail to do what they ought to do.

You see, men must work everyday -
It gives them a sense of accomplishment.
When men give an honest day's work
they stand a little taller,
speak more confidently,
and are grateful to earn each dollar.

Men must work and when they do
they provide for their family,
they plan, and prepare,
they have a purpose and direction,
and feel they are going somewhere.

When men are out of work,
sometimes they become lazy and selfish and stubborn.
Their confidence crumbles -
while the man staggers and stumbles,
pushing and trying against all odds,
to woo and impress the corporate gods.

But the men who work the least, I find,
are the men who think they have nothing to lose.
For sadly beginners are many,
and true enders are always too few,
because men will fail -
if they don't do what they know they were born to do.

157

The "No-Haggles"

There once was a town of "Haggles,"
who often haggled for fun.
They harraggled and harruseled
the homes of everyone.

Harry was a true haggler,
who hickled the haggard flock,
until one hick-up set him back
and knocked him off his block:

The "Haggles" decided to hang up their haggling,
to cease and desist - to be kind and do good.

Now this entire town of "No-Haggles,"
never would haggle, no not one.
They wouldn't haraggle or harrusel
the homes of anyone.

But Harry remained a haggler
and that once hickled, haggard flock,
reminded Harry that now all "No-Haggles"
were friendly, helpful, and would kindly talk.

But Harry wanted none of that
and continued in his haggling ways.
So Harry left the "No-Haggles" for good
and hasn't been heard from in days.

The Good Times and The Bad Times

The poet paints picturesque portraits
of perfection, and of defects,
of peace, and of war -
of love, and hate,
of what we've accomplished
and what we've never done before.

The good times and the bad times
blend together as one.
The virtues and each vice
that test and tempt each man,
compell, convince, persuade, perfect,
tear down, build up, restore, reject.

The Myth and The Moral
from the book
The "As If" Principle (motivational poetry)
by Jerald Simon

The man, the myth, and the moral,
  were walking through town one day.
The man told the myth about the moral,
  and then sent them both on their way.

The moral entered one town,
the myth into another,
and the man watched closely as time passed by.

The one town became productive,
  the other filled with perils and woes,
and the man can choose what he wants,
  and decides to which town he goes.

The Oak and the Acorn
from the book
The "As If" Principle (motivational poetry) (JS)

The oak and the acorn,
    stood side by side one day.
The tiny acorn marveled at the mighty oak
    and then quietly turned to say:

"Mighty Oak so tall and strong,
    so wise and old and grand.
How can a tiny acorn like me,
    rise up and take a stand?

"I'm just a tiny acorn,
    weak and timid and small,
but one day I want to be like you,
    majestic, mighty, and tall."

"My little, tiny acorn,"
    the great oak stately said,
"For now just be an acorn,
    don't try to jump ahead.

"Day by day you'll learn and grow,
    the wind will make you strong.
Reach for the sky, look to the light,
    and weather each storm when it comes along.

"Through snow, and rain, and thunderstorm,
which will badly beat you at times -
you'll gain experience, wisdom, and power,
    you'll improve and progress each day.
My tiny, little acorn,
    I have already paved the way."

The Little Train that Knew He Could
from the book
The "As If" Principle (motivational poetry) (JS)

The little train that thought he could,
   thought and thought all day.
But the little train that knew he could,
   was up and on his way.

The one began to strategize,
   to project and plan and prepare,
while the other simply went to work,
   and was quickly going somewhere.

The one who thought he could,
continued to think things through.
He thought of the struggles and the problems he'd face
and that if he'd fail, he'd have to live with disgrace.

He thought of the uphill battle before him,
   and the burden of the load he would bear,
and before he knew it, he decided to quit,
   and didn't want to go anywhere.

But the little train who knew he could,
   continued his climb each hour.
And the more he did, the better he felt,
   and was filled with ambition and power.

He climbed the hill with courage and might,
   overcame each obstacle he met.
And when he arrived at the top, he smiled,
   knowing that he'd never have to live with regret.

The Butterfiller and The Caterfly

from the book
The "As If" Principle (motivational poetry) (JS)

The butterfiller and the caterfly
were two of the most curious creatures.
The one, a butterfly, acted like a caterpillar,
while the other, a caterpillar, tried to fly like a butterfly.

The butterfly barely flitted, and never attempted to fly.
He was afraid of heights,
and would start to cry,
at the thought that he would, could, and should fly.

On the other hand, that caterpillar
knew he was destined to soar with the birds,
and never gave heed to the discouraging words;
from the ones who said he couldn't and wouldn't,
to the others who said he mustn't and shouldn't.

One day the caterfly disappeared
then emerged as a creature of flight;
the most beautiful butterfly any had seen,
transformed, as if during the night.

And the ones who said he couldn't and wouldn't,
and the others who said he mustn't and shouldn't,
watched in amazement as that butterfly flew -
higher than any tree ever grew.

The butterfiller and the caterfly
are two of the most curious creatures.
The one can fly and does not dare,
while the other dreams of going somewhere.

The Pebble and the Rock
from the book
The "As If" Principle (motivational poetry) (JS)

The pebble and the rock,
sat down and had a talk.
    The one complained of being small,
    the other that he was too tall.
Neither one seemed fully satisfied -
    they didn't seem happy at all.

The pebble and the rock,
often had this talk.
    They would gripe and whine,
    and waste their time,
complaining about what
they could not change.

The pebble and the rock,
decided never to talk.
    They argued that they
    were too different that day,
and sadly each one
    had nothing nice to say.

Several years passed
and the pebble and the rock
broke down and had another talk.
The one felt sorry for wasted time,
    the other that he'd been unkind.
They reclaimed their friendship
once and for all,
    and left their past behind.

Listen to an Old Man's Tale
from the book
The "As If" Principle (motivational poetry) (JS)

My brave, young, noble knight,
come listen to my tale.
Listen to an old man, who has seen far too many
young men get lost on life's trail.

Times have changed from what they were,
when knights were honest, noble, and pure -
when a man's word was more powerful than any deed,
and when noble knights helped those in need.

Listen to me reminisce about the past,
when faith was a power of substance and worth,
greater than any knowledge on earth.

Times do change, but have they changed for the better?
I believe they can and I believe they should.
I believe they will and I believe knights could -

Become noble knights, yet once again,
to inspire the souls of weakened men;
to be the example that men might be,
noble knights of dignity.

My brave, young, noble knight,
come listen to my tale.
Listen to an old man, who has seen far too many young men
get lost on life's trail.

We must be the example for each page and squire,
and shield and protect them from dangers on earth,
and help them have faith and know of their worth.

Sir Smile-a-lot
from the book
The "As If" Principle (motivational poetry) (JS)

Sir Smile-a-lot was a well known knight,
    with a smile stuck on his face.
He grinned and laughed and smiled a lot -
    such a friend to the human race.

When others were gloomy, depressed, or sad,
Sir Smile-a-lot smiled, and they'd feel glad.
    Each day was the same, and he'd smile a lot.
    He'd sing, and he'd laugh when others would not.

Then one day a sad little boy came walking his way.
"Sir Smile-a-lot", moaned the young little boy,
    "You smile a lot - I wish I could smile,
I don't even know how to smile.
I've never done it before,
    at least not in a long, long while."

This saddened Sir Smile-a-lot through and through,
for the first time ever, he knew not what to do.

He didn't feel like smiling,
    t'was the most depressing news he'd ever heard.
Then he noticed a beautiful flower,
    and heard the sweet song of a bird.

"Young boy", laughed the knight,
    as a smile reappeared,
"smiling is easy
    and shouldn't be feared."

"It's the first thing you should do
    when you awake each morn,
and the last item removed from
    the things that you've worn."

"Smell the flowers of life as you live it,
sing with the birds and hum with the bees.
    Smiling will help you be happy when sad,
and when others see you smile
    it will make them feel glad."

"Smile each day - never let your smile slip away,
    wear it with pride,
    never sulk, never hide.
Your smile is your shield,
it's your armor and strength.
    Smile every day
    and you'll help others on their way."

Pointers

These are a few of my favorite motivational quotes from some of the most influential men and women throughout history. These inspiring words of wisdom have motivated me to strive to be better, look for the good in every situation, and believe in myself and others. I hope these motivational messages help you as they have helped me.

You believe (and upon this little word *belief* hang all our sorrows and joys) that outward things have the power to make or mar your life; by so doing you submit to those outward things, confess that you are their slave, and they your unconditional master; by so doing, you invest them with a power which they do not, of themselves, possess, and you succumb, in reality, not to the mere circumstances, but to the gloom or gladness, the fear or hope, the strength or weakness, which your thought-sphere has thrown around them.

- James Allen

The significance of a man is not in what he attains but rather in what he longs to attain.

- Kahlil Gibran

It is never too late to be what you might have been.

- George Eliot

You must be the change you wish to see in the world.

- Mahatma Gandhi

The way to true riches is to enrich the soul by the acquisition of virtue.

- James Allen

Achievement is the knowledge that you have studied and worked hard and done the best that is in you. Success is being praised by others, and that's nice, too, but not as important or satisfying. Always aim for achievement and forget about success.

- Helen Hayes

Enthusiasm must be nourished with new actions, new aspirations, new efforts, new vision. It is one's own fault if his enthusiasm is gone; he has failed to feed it.

- Papyrus

It is a mark of intelligence, no matter what you are doing, to have a good time doing it.

- B.W. Cochran

Ninety-nine percent of the failures come from people who have the habit of making excuses.

- George W. Carver

Your purpose in life is to find your purpose in life and give your whole heart to it.

- Buddha

All men who have turned out worth anything have had the chief hand in their own education.

- Sir Walter Scott

A man is never beaten until he thinks he is.

- Charles Gow

Our greatest weakness lies in giving up. The most certain way to succeed is always to try just one more time.

- Thomas Edison

It is not work that kills men; it is worry. Work is healthy, and you can hardly put more upon a man than he can bear; but worry is rust upon the blade. It is not the revolution that destroys the machinery, it is the friction.

- Henry Ward Beecher

If people knew how hard I have had to work to gain my mastery, it wouldn't seem wonderful at all.

- Michelangelo

Beaten paths are for beaten men.

- Eric Johnston

Merit begets confidence, confidence begets enthusiasm, enthusiasm conquers the world.

- Walter Cottingham

I never blame failure - there are too many complicated situations in life - but I am absolutely merciless toward lack of effort.

- F. Scott Fitzgerald

Decide what you want and write your goals. Then convert your goals into positive, present tense statements called affirmations. Affirm your goals each day until they become part of your subconscious mechanism.

- Anonymous

I believe that anyone can conquer fear by doing the thing he fears to do, provided he keeps doing them until he gets a record of successful experiences behind him.

- Eleanor Roosevelt

First say to yourself what you would be; and then do what you have to do.

- Epictetus

The greatest discovery of my generation is that human beings can alter their lives by altering their attitudes of mind.

- William James

Few men during their lifetime come anywhere near exhausting the resources dwelling within them. There are deep wells of strength that are never used.

- Richard E. Byrd

There is no royal road to anything. One thing at a time, and all things in succession. That which grows slowly endures.

- J.G. Holland

Nothing in the world can take the place of persistence. Talent will not; nothing is more common than unsuccessful men with talent. Genius will not; unrewarded genius is almost a proverb. Education will not; the world is full of educated derelicts. Persistence and determination alone are omnipotent.

- Calvin Coolidge

Adversity introduces a man to himself.

- Anonymous

There are really only three types of people: those who make things happen, those who watch things happen, and those who say, "what happened?"

- Ann Landers

You will never "find" time for anything. If you want time, you must make it.

- Charles Bixton

Men often become what they believe themselves to be. If I believe I cannot do something, it makes me incapable of doing it. But when I believe I can, then I acquire the ability to do it even if I don't have it in the beginning.

- Mahatma Gandhi

The average person puts 25% of his energy and ability into his work. The world takes off its hat to those who put in more than 50% of their capacity, and stands on its head for the few and far between souls who devote 100%.

- Andrew Carnegie

When a man can put a limit on what he will do, he has put a limit on what he can do.

- Charles M. Schwab

We grow great by dreams. All big men are dreamers. They see things in the soft haze of a spring day or in the red fire of a long winter's evening. Some of us let these dreams die, but others nourish and protect them, nurse them through bad days till they bring them to the sunshine and light which comes always to those who sincerely hope that their dreams will come true.

- Woodrow Wilson

Seize this very minute;
what you can do or dream
you can do, begin it;
Boldness has genius, power
and magic in it.
Only engage and then
the mind grows heated;
Begin and the work
will be completed.

- Goethe

A pessimist is one who makes difficulties of his opportunities; an optimist is one who makes opportunities of his difficulties.

- Reginald B. Mansell

The unexamined life is not worth living.

- Socrates

Genius is one percent inspiration and ninety-nine percent perspiration. I never did anything worth doing by accident, nor did any of my inventions come by accident, they came by work.

- Thomas Edison

A person who never made a mistake never tried anything new.

- Albert Einstein

Do all the good you can
by all the means you can
In all the ways you can
In all the places you can
at all the times you can
to all the people you can
as long as ever you can.

- John Wesley

Why build these cities glorious if man unbuilded goes? In vain we build the world, unless the builder also grows.

- Edwin Markham

God helps those who help themselves.

- Benjamin Franklin

A man's manners are a mirror in which he shows his portrait.

- Johann Wolfgang von Goethe

We receive three educations, one from our parents, one from our school masters, and one from the world. The third contradicts all that the first two teach us.

- Charles Louis de Secondat,
Baron de Montesqieu

All that Adam had, all that Caesar could, you have and can do...Build, therefore, your own world.

- Ralph Waldo Emerson

Well begun is half done.

- Aristotle

It is the lone worker who makes the first advance in a subject; the details may be worked out by a team, but the prime idea is due to enterprise, thought, and perception of an individual.

- Alexander Flemming

We either find a way, or make one.

- Hannibal

The longer I live the more convinced I become that God governs in the affairs of men. And have we now forgotten that powerful friend? Or do we imagine we no longer need his assistance.

- Benjamin Franklin

I have only just a minute.
Only sixty seconds in it.
Forced upon me, can't refuse it,
didn't seek it, didn't choose it.
But it's up to me to use it,
I must suffer if I lose it,
give account if I abuse it.
Just one tiny little minute,
but eternity is in it.

- Dr. Benjamin E. Mays

Every truth passes through three stages before it is recognized. In the first, it is ridiculed, in the second it is opposed, in the third it is regarded as self-evident.

- Arthur Schopenhauer

Dost thou love life? Then do not squander time. For that's the stuff life is made of.

- Benjamin Franklin

The most difficult thing is the decision to act, the rest is merely tenacity. The fears are paper tigers. You can do anything you decide to do. You can act to change and control your life; and the procedure, the process is its own reward.

- Amelia Earhart

Nothing great was ever achieved without enthusiasm.

- Ralph Waldo Emerson

One's own self is well hidden from one's own self; of all mines of treasure, one's own is the last to be dug up.

- Friedrich Wilhem Nietzsche

Blessed is the man who, having nothing to say, abstains from giving in words evidence of the fact.

- George Eliot Sands (Marian Evans Cross)

We must not promise what we ought not, lest we be called on to perform what we cannot.

- Abraham Lincoln

The highest stage in moral ure at which we can arrive is when we recognize that we ought to control our thoughts.

- Charles Darwin

One can choose to go back toward safety or forward toward growth. Growth must be chosen again and again, fear must be overcome again and again.

- Abraham Maslow

It is not the strongest of the species that survive, nor the most intelligent, but the one most responsive to change.

- Charles Darwin

By prevailing over all obstacles and distractions, one may unfailingly arrive at his chosen goal or destination.

- Christopher Columbus

And in the end it's not the years in your life that count. It's the life in your years.

- Abraham Lincoln

Imagination is more important than knowledge.

- Albert Einstein

Better to remain silent and be thought a fool than to speak out and remove all doubt.

- Abraham Lincoln

I am not afraid of an army of lions led by a sheep; I am afraid of an army of sheep led by a lion.

- Alexander the Great

If I have a thousand ideas and only one turns out to be good, I am satisfied.

- Alfred Nobel

I destroy my enemy when I make him my friend.

- Abraham Lincoln

There is nothing impossible to him who will try.

- Alexander the Great

Concentrate all your thoughts upon the work at hand. The sun's rays do not burn until brought to a focus.

- Alexander Graham Bell

I do not feel obliged to believe that the same God who has endowed us with sense, reason, and intellect has intended us to forgo their use.

- Galileo Galilei

People begin to become successful the minute they decide to be.

- Archimedes

Holding on to anger is like grasping a hot coal with the intent of throwing it at someone else; you are the one who gets burned.

- Gautama Buddha

He is able who thinks he is able.

- Gautama Buddha

Many people may listen, but few people actually hear.

- Archimedes

Never leave that till tomorrow which you can do today.

- Benjamin Franklin

Education is the best provision for the journey to old age.

- Aristotle

I have never met a man so ignorant that I couldn't learn something from him.

- Galileo Galilei

Do not anticipate trouble or worry about what may never happen. Keep in the sunlight.

- Benjamin Franklin

Do not dwell in the past, do not dream of the future, concentrate the mind on the present moment.

- Gautama Buddha

A man who dares to waste one hour of time has not discovered the value of life.

- Charles Darwin

All truths are easy to understand once they are discovered; the point is to discover them.

- Galileo Galilei

There are fashions in reading, even in thinking. You don't have to follow them unless you want to. On the other hand, watch out. Don't stick too closely to your favorite subject. That would keep you from adventuring into other fields. It's silly to build a wall around your interests.

- Walt Disney

You cannot teach a man anything; you can only help him discover it in himself.

- Galileo Galilei

Procrastination is the thief of time.

- Edward Young

Things do not change; we change.

- Henry David Theoreau

Circumstances do not determine a man, they reveal him.

- James Allen

Every man becomes, to a certain degree, what the people he generally converses with are.

- Lord Philip Dormer Stanhope Chesterfield

An idea that is developed and put into action is more important than an idea that exists only as an idea.

- Gautama Buddha

All the adversity I've had in my life, all my troubles and obstacles, have strengthened me...You may not realize it when it happens, but a kick in the teeth may be the best thing in the world for you.

- Walt Disney

Time is money.

- Benjamin Franklin

Worry is the interest paid by those who borrow trouble.

- George Washington

If everyone is moving forward together then success takes care of itself.

- Henry Ford

You can tell the character of every man when you see how he receives praise.

- Lucius Annaeus Seneca

A wise man's questions contain half the answer.

- Gabirol (Solomon ben Yehunda ibn Gabirol)

Somehow I can't believe there are any heights that can't be scaled by a man who knows the secret of making dreams come true. This special secret, it seems to me, can be summarized in four C's. They are curiosity, confidence, courage, and constancy and the greatest of those is confidence. When you believe a thing, believe it all the way, implicitly and unquestionably.

- Walt Disney

Man is what he believes.

- Anton Pavtovich Chekhov

There will never be a system invented which will do away with the necessity for work.

- Henry Ford

Clear your mind of can't.

- Dr. Samuel Johnson

Chop your own wood, and it will warm you twice.

- Henry Ford

Our heritage and ideas, our code and standards - the things we live by and teach our children - are preserved and diminished by how freely we exchange ideas and feelings.

- Walt Disney

The father who does not teach his son his duties is equally guilty with the son who neglects them.

- Confucious

Whether you think you can or whether you think you can't, you're right.

- Henry Ford

The way to get started is to quit talking and begin doing.

- Walt Disney

Failure is the opportunity to begin again more intelligently.

- Henry Ford

A person should set his goals as early as he can and devote all his energy and talent to getting there. With enough effort, he may achieve it. Or he may find something that is even more rewarding. But in the end, no matter what the outcome, he will know he has been alive.

- Walt Disney

Ultimately, the only power to which man should aspire is that which he exercises over himself.

- Elie Wiesel

Curiosity is the wick in the candle of learning.

- William Arthur Ward

A man is but the product of his thoughts. What he thinks, he becomes.

- Anonymous

All our dreams can come true...if we have the courage to pursue them.

- Walt Disney

Treat a man as he appears to be, and you make him worse. But treat a man as if he were what he potentially could be, and you make him what he should be.

- Johann Wolfgang von Goethe

It is more noble by silence to avoid an injury than by argument to overcome it.

- Francis Beaumont

An invasion of armies can be resisted, but not an idea whose time has come.

- Victor Hugo

Would you live with ease, do what you ought, and not what you please.

- Benjamin Franklin

No one can make you feel inferior without your consent.

- Eleanor Roosevelt

We keep moving forward, opening new doors, and doing new things, because we're curious and curiosity keeps leading us down new paths.

- Walt Disney

They can do all because they think they can.

- Virgil

He who conquers others is strong. He who conquers himself is mighty.

- Lao Tzu

Knowledge is power.

- Francis Bacon

Read the best books first, or you may not have a chance to read them at all.

- Henry David Thoreau

I can never stand still. I must explore and experiment. I am never satisfied with my work. I resent the limitations of my own imagination.

- Walt Disney

Get a good idea and stay with it. Dog it, and work it until it's done and done right.

- Walt Disney

If you can dream it, you can do it.

- Walt Disney

In seeking wisdom thou art wise; in imagining that thou hast attained it thou are a fool.

- Rabbi Ben-Azai

Trust men and they will be true to you. Treat them greatly, and they will show themselves great.

- Ralph Waldo Emerson

The greatest revolution in our generation is that of human beings, who by changing the inner attitudes of their minds, can change the outer aspects of their lives.

- Marilyn Ferguson

I am only one, but I am one. I can not do everything, but I can do something. And I will not let what I can not do interfere with what I can do.

- Edward E. Hale

The greatest use of life is to spend it for something that will outlast it.

- William James

Sooner or later everyone sits down to a banquet of consequences.

- Robert Louis Stephenson

Imagination grows by exercise and contrary to common belief is more powerful in the mature than in the young.

- Anonymous

We hold these truths to be self evident: that all men are created equal; that they are endowed by their creator with certain unalienable rights; that among these are life, liberty, and the pursuit of happiness.

- Thomas Jefferson

For all sad words of tongue and pen, the saddest are these, "it might have been."

- John Greenleaf Whittier

Early to bed and early to rise, makes a man healthy, wealthy, and wise.

- Benjamin Franklin

He does not preach what he practices till he has practiced what he preaches.

- Confucius

I think that much of the advice given to young men about saving money is wrong. I never saved a cent until I was forty years old. I invested in myself - in study, in mastering my tools, in preparation. Many a man who is putting a few dollars a week into the bank would do much better to put it into himself.

- Henry Ford

It is very important to generate a good attitude, a good heart, as much as possible. From this, happiness in both the short term and the long term for both yourself and others will come.

- Dalai Lama

For every minute you're angry, you lose sixty seconds of happiness.

- Ralph Waldo Emerson

It isn't enough to talk about peace. One must believe in it. And it isn't enough to believe it. One must work at it.

- Eleanor Roosevelt

Watch your thoughts; they become words.
Watch your words; they become actions.
Watch your actions; they become habits.
Watch your habits; they become character.
Watch your character; it becomes your destiny.

- Frank Outlaw

Intellectual growth should commence at birth and cease only at death.

- Albert Einstein

Ignorance, the root and the stem of every evil.

- Plato

They that won't be counseled, can't be helped.

- Benjamin Franklin (Poor Richard)

It is the mark of an educated mind to be able to entertain a thought without accepting it.

- Aristotle

You can make more friends in two months by becoming interested in other people than you can in two years by trying to get other people interested in you.

- Dale Carnegie

Music is a moral law. It gives soul to the universe, wings to the mind, flight to the imagination, and charm and gaiety to life and to everything.

- Plato

Music expresses that which cannot be said and on which it is impossible to be silent.

- Victor Hugo

The best way to cheer yourself up is to cheer somebody else up.

- Mark Twain

Most folks are about as happy as they make up their minds to be.

- Abraham Lincoln

Education's purpose is to replace an empty mind with an open one.

- Malcolm Forbes

Everything has its beauty, but not everyone sees it.

- Confucius

Peace comes from within. Do not seek it without.

- Buddha

Success is walking from failure to failure with no loss of enthusiasm.

- Winston Churchill

Music in the soul can be heard by the universe.

- Lao Tzu

Success is dependent on effort.

- Sophocles

We are what we repeatedly do. Excellence then is not an act but a habit.

- Aristotle

Opportunity is missed by most people, because it is dressed in overalls and looks like work.

- Thomas Edison

I do not agree with what you have to say, but I'll defend to the death your right to say it.

- Voltaire

No man is a failure who has friends.

- From "It's a Wonderful Life" starring James Stewart

It is our attitude at the beginning of a difficult task which, more than anything else, will affect its successful outcome.

- William James

Try not to become a man of success, but rather try to become a man of value.

- Albert Einstein

We become what we think about.

- Earl Nightingale

The optimist sees opportunity in every danger; the pessimist sees danger in every opportunity.

- Winston Churchill

Believe and succeed.

- Earl Nightingale

Be not afraid of life. Believe that life is worth living and your belief will help create the fact.

- William James

197

Finish each day and be done with it. You have done what you could. Some blunders and absurdities no doubt crept in; forget them as soon as you can. Tomorrow is a new day; begin it well and serenely and with too high a spirit to be cumbered with your old nonsense.

- Ralph Waldo Emerson

Nothing can stop the man with the right mental attitude from achieving his goal; nothing on earth can help the man with the wrong mental attitude.

- Thomas Jefferson

Our attitude toward life determines life's attitude towards us.

- Earl Nightingale

Thinking is the hardest work there is. That is why so few people engage in it.

- Henry Ford

All you need is the plan, the road map, and the courage to press on to your destination.

- Earl Nightingale

Where there is sterling faith and uncompromising purity there is health, there is success, there is power. In such a one, disease, failure, and disaster can find no lodgment, for there is nothing on which they can feed.

- James Allen

One ought, everyday at least, to hear a little song, read a good poem, see a fine picture, and if it were possible, to speak a few reasonable words.

- Johann Wolfgang Von Goethe

All men's accomplishments were first wrought out in thought, and then objectivized. The author, inventor, the architect first builds up his work in thought, and having perfected it in all its parts as a complete and harmonious whole upon the thought-plane, he then commences to materialize it, to bring it down to the material or sense-plane.

- James Allen

Everybody is a genius. But if you judge a fish by its ability to climb a tree it will live its whole life believing that it is stupid.

- Albert Einstein

He who has conquered self has conquered the universe.

- James Allen

You cannot bring prosperity by discouraging thrift.
You cannot help small men by tearing down big men.
You cannot strengthen the weak by weakening the strong.
You cannot lift the wage earner by pulling down the wage payer.
You cannot help the poor by destroying the rich.
You cannot keep out of trouble by spending more than your income.
You cannot further brotherhood of men by inciting class hatred.
You cannot establish security on borrowed money.
You cannot build character and courage by taking away man's initiative and independence.
You cannot help men permanently by doing for them what they could and should do for themselves.

- Rev. William J.H. Boetcker

Circumstances can only affect you in so far as you allow them to do so.

- James Allen

Change your thoughts and you change your world.

- Norman Vincent Peale

Do you wish for kindness? Be Kind.
Do you ask for truth? Be true.
What you give of yourself you find;
Your world is a reflex of you.

- James Allen

Don't judge each day by the harvest you reap but by the seeds that you plant.

- Robert Louis Stevenson

You may bring about that improved condition in your outward life which you desire, if you will unswervingly resolve to improve your inner life.

- James Allen

Gratitude is the fairest blossom which springs from the soul.

- Henry Ward Beecher

Happiness resides not in possessions, and not in gold, happiness dwells in the soul.

- Democritus

If you would become truly and permanently prosperous, you must first become virtuous. It is therefore unwise to aim directly at prosperity, to make it the one object of life, to reach out greedily for it. To do this is to ultimately defeat yourself. But rather aim at self-perfection, make useful and unselfish service the object of your life, and ever reach out hands of faith toward the supreme and unalterable good.

- James Allen

Hope is a waking dream.

- Aristotle

Lust, hatred, anger, vanity, pride, covetousness, self-indulgence, self seeking, obstinacy - all these are poverty and weakness, whereas, love, purity, gentleness, meekness, patience, compassion, generosity, self-forgetfulness, and self-renunciation - all these are wealth and power.

- James Allen

In a gentle way, you can shake the world.

- Mahatma Gandhi

The glory of friendship is not the outstretched hand, nor the kindly smile, nor the joy of companionship; it's the spiritual inspiration that comes to one when he discovers that someone else believes in him and is willing to trust him with his friend.

- Ralph Waldo Emerson

To follow, under all circumstances, the highest promptings within you; to be always true to the divine self, to rely upon the inward light, the inward voice, and to pursue your purpose with a fearless and restful heart, believing that the future will yield unto you the meed of every thought and effort; knowing that the laws of the universe can never fail, and that your own will come back to you with mathematical exactitude, this is faith and the living of faith. By the power of such faith the dark waters of uncertainty are divided, every mountain of difficulty crumbles away, and the believing soul passes on unharmed.

- James Allen

Nothing will ever be attempted, if all possible objections must be first overcome.

- Dr. Samuel Johnson

Nothing is more terrible than ignorance in action.

- Johann Wolfgang von Goethe

We're drowning in information and starving for knowledge.

- Rutherford D. Rogers

The fool doth think he is wise, but the wise man knows himself to be a fool.

- William Shakespeare

The only difference between the saint and the sinner is that every saint has a past, and every sinner has a future.

- Oscar Wilde

In nature, there are neither rewards nor punishments; there are consequences.

- Robert Greene Ingersoll

To one who has faith, no explanation is necessary. To one without faith, no explanation is possible.

- St. Thomas Aquinas

As a well-spent day brings happy sleep, so a life well used brings happy death.

- Leonardo da Vinci

You cannot do a kindness too soon, for you never know how soon it will be too late.

- Ralph Waldo Emerson

Not by age but by capacity is wisdom acquired.

- Titus Maccius Plautus

We judge ourselves by what we feel capable of doing, while others judge us by what we have already done.

- Henry Wadsworth Longfellow

The time is always right to do what is right.

- Martin Luther King, Jr.

A man who has to be convinced to act before he acts is not a man of action...You must act as you breathe.

- George Clemenceau

The efforts which we make to escape from our destiny only serve to lead us into it.

- Ralph Waldo Emerson

We may affirm absolutely that nothing great in the world has been accomplished without passion.

- Georg Wilhelm Friedrich Hegel

Prejudice is the child of ignorance.

- William Hazlitt

Few things help an individual more than to place responsibility upon him and to let him know that you trust him.

- Booker T. Washington

No great man ever complains of want of opportunity.

- Ralph Waldo Emerson

Our doubts are traitors, and make us lose the good we oft might win, by fearing to attempt.

- William Shakespeare

A certain amount of opposition is a great help to a man. Kites rise against, not with the wind.

- John Neal

This, then, is the secret of health - a pure heart and a well-ordered mind; this is the secret of success - an unfaltering faith, and a wisely-directed purpose; and to rein in, with unfaltering will the dark steed of desire, this is the secret of power.

- James Allen

He who mistrusts most should be trusted least.

- Theognis

A life being very short, and the quiet hours of it few, we ought to waste none of them in reading valueless books.

- John Ruskin

The investigation of the meaning of words is the beginning of education.

- Antisthenes

What does not destroy me makes me stronger.

- Friedrich Wilhelm Nietzsche

Would you persuade, speak of interest, not reason.

- Benjamin Franklin

What it lies in our power to do, it lies in our power not to do.

- Aristotle

Men of genius do not excel in any profession because they labor in it, but they labor in it because they excel.

- William Hazlitt

It is worse still to be ignorant of your ignorance.

- Saint Jerome

Language most shows a man; speak that I may see thee.

- Ben Johnson

The man who does not read good books has no advantage over the man who can't read them.

- Mark Twain (Samuel Longhorne Clemens)

Well-timed silence hath more eloquence than speech.

- Martin Farquhar Tupper

Adversity has the effect of eliciting talents which, in prosperous circumstances, would have lain dormant.

- Horace (Quintus Haratius Faccus)

Each of us in our own way and in our own occupation can become a genius, even if unrecognized as such by society. To be a genius simply means to do what you enjoy doing. This is the true genius of life. Mediocrity is never daring to do what you love, for fear of what others will say or for fear of losing your security.

- Mark Fisher (from The Instant Millionaire)

Mere wishing brings nothing but disappointment; it is living that tells. The foolish wish and grumble; the wise work and wait.

- James Allen

Seven dangers to human virtue:

1. Wealth without work
2. Pleasure without conscience
3. Knowledge without character
4. Business without ethics
5. Science without humanity
6. Religion without sacrifice
7. Politics without principle

- Mahatma Gandhi

Book Jerald as a Presenter/Performer for your next event:

Contact: Suzanne
jeraldsimon@musicmotivation.com
seminars@musicmotivation.com

Below is a list of some of the speaking and performing events Jerald has done and is willing to do.

We can customize to your specific needs.

Speaking and Performing at Events:

Workshops, Seminars, Music Camps, and Concerts (i.e. Concerts/Mini Concerts, Corporate Events/Parties/Dinners, Schools, Youth Groups, Recitals, MTNA Conventions and Conferences, MTNA Chapter Meetings, other Music Organizations, Schools, Groups, etc., Workshops, Summer Camps, Devotionals and Firesides, and any of the following:

Anniversaries, Awards Nights, Banquets, Birthday Parties, Children's Birthday Parties, Celebrations, Christmas Parties, Church Services, Clubs, Community Events, Conventions, Corporate Functions, Country Clubs, Cruise Ships, Dinner Dances, Festivals, Fund Raisers, Funerals, Graduation Parties, Grand Openings, Hotels, Jingles, Movie Sound tracks, Picnic, Private Parties, Proms, Resorts, Restaurants, Reunions, Showers, Studio Session, TV Sound tracks, Weddings, and customizable performances to meet your personal needs).

Book Jerald as the next Speaker/Entertainer for your next event! Motivate those who attend the event with Music Motivation®! Music Motivation® Workshops, Seminars, and Music Camps are focused on Theory Therapy, Innovative Improvisation, and Creative Composition with a Music Mentor. The emphasis is on teaching music students with "Music that excites, entertains, and educates". If you are interested in becoming a Music Motivation® Mentor, please email Music Motivation® at musicmentor@musicmotivation.com . If you would like to book Jerald Simon as the Music Mentor presenter or motivational speaker for your next event (i.e. recital, MTNA chapter meetings, workshops, summer camps, devotionals and firesides, corporate events, etc.) Please email Music Motivation®.

Booking Jerald is subject to his availability and waiting list.

Music Motivation®

http://musicmotivation.com

"Cool music that excites, entertains, and educates."
"Let music motivate you!"

The Music Motivation® website was created as a resource for music teachers (primarily piano teachers), music students (primarily piano students) and parents. The focus is on making music fun, exciting, entertaining, and educational. We noticed a problem: "How do we keep kids excited and motivated to continue with their music lessons - especially teenagers?" Here was a question we had and a solution we thought might work:

PROBLEM: How do you motivate boys (teenage boys in particular) to want to play the piano or keep playing the piano? What works?

SOLUTION: Let them play cool sounding music - The Cool Songs for Cool Kids Series (pre-primer, primer, books 1, 2, & 3) and Cool Songs that ROCK books 1 and 2

visit the following areas of the
Music Motivation® website for **FREE resources:**

FANS: **http://musicmotivation.com/fans**
MUSIC TEACHERS: **http://musicmotivation.com/musicteachers**
MUSIC STUDENTS: **http://musicmotivation.com/musicstudents**
PARENTS: **http://musicmotivation.com/parents**

Subscribe to Jerald's YouTube Channel:
http://youtube.com/jeraldsimon for weekly piano videos on learning and playing the piano: Fun to Play! Videos (piano lessons with Jerald)

Be sure to **subscribe to The Music Motivation® newsletter.**
(We will not sell or share your information)

The three main areas of focus for Music Motivation® are: Theory Therapy, Innovative Improvisation, and Creative Composition.

Music Motivation® Goal: Make music lessons (primarily piano lessons) cool, exciting, entertaining, and educational.

Music Motivation® Goal (for music educators): One of our primary goals at Music Motivation® is to help prepare the next generation of composers, arrangers, musicians, music teachers, and musicologists to use their music and their love of music to make a difference in their own lives, their community, and the world.

I have several CDs of original music I have composed that I would love to have you listen to. You can listen to my music on Spotify, Pandora, etc., or purchase my music on iTunes, Amazon, and all on-line music stores. I compose several different styles from hymn arrangements to meditation music, new age piano solos to pop, techno-pop, rock, and even scary Halloween music. Let me know what you think of my music!

Available from all online music stores.
Many albums are also available on
Spotify and Pandora. Enjoy the music!

Every month I produce and release a new **"Cool Song"** available for all piano students and piano teachers on my website (musicmotivation.com). Each new "Cool Song" is emailed to Music Motivation® mentees (piano teachers and piano students) according to their preferred subscription. See which subscription is the best fit for you and for your piano students (if you are a piano teacher) by visiting: http://musicmotivation.com/annualsubscription. I also comes out with **Theory Tip Tuesday** videos.

I have also created 21 music books of original piano solos - most with music backing tracks of other instruments and sounds. In total there are over 250 fun piano solos between the 21 books from pre-primer to advanced level pieces that have been composed primarily to motivate teenage boys to play the piano! Visit **musicmotivation.com/musicbooksbyjerald** to learn more.

Check out these best sellers by Jerald Simon

Poetry Books by Jerald Simon

Other poetry books by **Jerald Simon**:

* **Motivational Poetry** * **Poetry Smoetry** * **Season of Life**

A Brief Message from Jerald to Piano Students and Parents...

If you come to piano lessons each week and walk away from your lessons and only learn about music notation, rhythm, and dots on a page, then I have failed as a Music Mentor. Life lessons are just as important, if not more important, than music lessons. I would rather have you learn more about goal setting and achieving, character, dedication, and personal improvement. To have you learn to love music, appreciate it, and play it, is a wonderful by-product you will have for the rest of your life - a talent that will enrich your life and the lives of others. To become a better musician is wonderful and important, but *to become a better person is more important.*

As a Music Mentor I want to mentor students to be the very best they can be. If you choose not to practice, you essentially choose not to improve. This is true in any area of life. Everyone has the same amount of time allotted to them. What you choose to do with your time, and where you spend your time, has little to do with the activities being done and more to do with the value attached to each activity.

I believe it's important to be well-rounded and have many diverse interests. I want students to enjoy music, to learn to be creative and understand how to express themselves musically - either by creating music of their own, or interpreting the music of others - by arranging and improvising well known music. In addition, I encourage students to play sports, dance, sing, draw, read, and develop their talents. I want them to be more than musicians, I want them to learn to become well-rounded complete individuals.

Above all, I want everyone to continually improve and do their best no matter what they do or choose to do. I encourage everyone to set goals, dream big, and be the best they can be in whatever they choose to do. Life is full of wonderful choices. Choose the best out of life and learn as much as you can from everyone - everywhere. I prefer being called a Music Mentor because I want to mentor others and help them to live their dreams.

Your life is your musical symphony. Make it a masterpiece!

215

Make the most of each minute!

This is the last page of this book, but it is the beginning of a new day for you and for me. Every day that comes our way is pure, free from mistakes, perfect. It only becomes imperfect if we allow ourselves to get in the way and mess things up. We can make the most of each minute we have by focusing on doing our best right now. Don't worry about what is on the horizon. Take it into consideration as how you can prepare right now for what is to come, but stay in the moment and enjoy everything right now.

Life is too short to get tangled up in the tragedies of tomorrow. Be happy this hour. It's a new day for change, growth, improvement, happiness, love, laughter, and giving. Every second should be sacred because they add up to more than minutes - they add up to memories. Make the most of each moment and make good memories. Make great memories. Life should be about learning and growing, but in addition to being meaningful, it should and must be memorable.

If you slip up and get down on yourself, as we all do, it's okay. Start over every second with a clean slate and a glad attitude. You can refer to it as your gladitude.

Look in the mirror and tell yourself you love yourself. Be honest and sincere and mean it. It's more than learning to like yourself, which you must do, it's about loving your strengths, accepting your weaknesses and being willing to work on them, and letting go of any unrealistic expectations of yourself. Your future is bright and beautiful, and wonderful.

I'm excited for your future and I'm excited for mine. We are both on a wonderful journey of self discovery, personal growth, some heartache and pain here and there, but overall we will triumph! We are stronger than our sorrows. We are working together on being the very best we can be because we believe in each other. We hope for the best that is in each other. We pray for each other and know that together we can do great things in life because we can bring out the best in each other.

Love life! Live it to the fullest and be actively engaged in helping others as you help yourself. I know God will bless you and help you through the good times and the bad times of life. Have faith. Have hope. Have an outlook of optimism in all that you do and you will continually be happy because you see the happiness around you and strive to help others be happy as well!

Be Happy! Smile all the while and be your best!

- JERALD